Pr

Mind

"In this book Sheri has taken the best of the Toltec teachings and made them her own, reorganized them and created her own mythology. Using humor and her scientific background she has designed a method for people, no matter where they are located, to experience the Toltec work and to build onto the teachings I originally presented in 'The Four Agreements®.'"

— Don Miguel Ruiz, author of *The Four Agreements®*

"Loving life is our choice. Dr. Rosenthal has dedicated the attention, time and energy necessary to transform her life from what she inherited as the way to live to an authentic life of inspiration and compassion. There is no greater gift to creation than our willingness to transform ourselves from suffering and fear to love and freedom. This book is a road map to that journey. Travel well."

— Lee McCormick author of *The Spirit Recovery Meditation Journal: Meditations for Reclaiming Your Authenticity* and founder/co-owner of The Recovery Ranch

"Banish Mind Spam!' is a humorous and engaging book that will help you move past any needless stories you tell yourself about 'how it is' that stand in your way keeping you from achieving your hopes, goals and dreams."

— Ray Dodd, author of *The Power of Belief*, and *BeliefWorks*

"Banish Mind Spam!' is a masterpiece. This is the perfect guidebook to free your mind of the programming that results in emotional anguish and suffering. Allow Sheri to be your guide to banish your Mind Spam and experience the joys of personal freedom and love. This is a must have book to read, use and share with everyone you know."

— Susyn Reeve M.Ed., author of *Choose Peace & Happiness*, *The Gift of the Acorn*, and co-creator of *WithForgiveness*

## *More praise ...*

"*Sheri writes with grace, humor, wisdom, and love. Let her guide you into the recesses of your own mind, where you'll discover how to rewire your life for happiness beyond your wildest dreams.*"

— Brandt Morgan, author of *Vision Walk: Asking Questions,
Getting Answers, Shifting Consciousness*

"*Sheri Rosenthal has done it again! In 'Banish Mind Spam!' she has brought ancient and modern wisdoms into a common sense manual for reprogramming your mind's computer. And the goal? Simply to be happy. What more could we ask? Using the model of a computer and its program, Dr. Rosenthal has simplified the understanding of how our beliefs and agreements control our lives. With her many examples and actions steps, she shows the way to understanding and reprogramming those beliefs, and 'upgrading the program.' Thorough lists of core beliefs on many different subjects offer we readers a format for beginning the exploration of the hidden parts of our minds. And throughout the book, Dr. Rosenthal reminds us that unconditional love for ourselves and all of creation is the key to the happiness that cannot be taken away from us. Overall, this book is a good read for beginning and experienced travelers on the road to freedom from their Mind Spam, and to a fulfilling new life based on love and acceptance. I recommend it highly.*"

— Allan Hardman, Toltec Master, author of
*The Everything Toltec Wisdom Book*

"*Banish Mind Spam' is THE mind manual I wish all of us would have been gifted with at birth. Imagine if we were all handed an owner's manual for our mind when we first learned to read! Ah, what a different world it would be. Sheri's piercing clarity and love shines through every page. Her newest book lovingly guides us into the crooks and crevices of our mind, and with humor and a firm hand teaches us how to release the old programming and claim our mind's pure grace. I will recommend this book to all my students and friends.*

— Heather Ash Amara, author of *The Four Elements of Change,
The Toltec Tarot*, and co-author of *Spiritual Integrity* with Raven Smith.

# Mind *Banish* Spam!

*Four Steps For Deprogramming*
*Self-Limiting And Self-Sabotaging Beliefs*

Sheri A. Rosenthal, DPM

WARRIOR'S PATH PRESS
GULFPORT, FLORIDA

*Also by Sheri A. Rosenthal, DPM:*

*The Complete Idiot's Guide to Toltec Wisdom*

Published by Warrior's Path Press
6860 Gulfport Blvd. Box 173
South Pasadena, FL 33707

Editing: Michelle Hagen
Cover Art: Ted Raess
Layout Design: Peggy Raess

**Library of Congress Control Number: 2008920722**

ISBN 9780981478104

*This book is dedicated to all the people
in my life who have blessed me with their
unending and unconditional love.*

# Table of Contents

# Foreword

*I remember meeting Sheri back in 1997* on her first Power Journey to Teotihuacán. She was in the process of selling her medical practice and was stressed, confused and unhappy with her life, like so many people these days. Sheri was frightened, apprehensive, angry and very defensive! But she was so focused on changing herself that she was able to take a chance and open to the magic of the experience available to her. It was beautiful to watch her expand and see the possibilities of herself for the first time in her life and open to the unconditional love that she truly was. There was something about her that was very determined and I knew she would become one of my apprentices who would vigorously pursue her personal freedom.

Over the years I have watched a difficult, stubborn, "don't tell me what to do" physician turn into a beautiful and loving Nagual woman of power. And what an amazing process that has been to behold! I had the opportunity to work very closely with her during the period of time when she was my business manager and executive director of Sixth Sun Foundation. During this juncture I was able to observe her teaching skills grow and blossom as she mastered the impeccability of the word. Finally with my blessing and love, I encouraged her to leave my organization and share her great gift with others. If you haven't had the opportunity to hear her share herself, please take advantage of it, as she has so much experience, wisdom and love to offer!

Sheri has been such a force in our Toltec community. Some years ago she inspired me to offer Toltec dreaming, a class I never thought many students would be interested in taking. Her yearning to learn and grow created the opportunity for hundreds of people to experience dreaming and the Mastery of Intent. To be honest, she haunted me relentlessly with her enthusiasm and desire to be free until I agreed to teach the class. She truly has made her personal freedom and the expression of Spirit her life's path — both for herself and others.

In this book Sheri has taken the best of the Toltec teachings and made them her own, reorganized them and created her own mythology.

Using humor and her scientific background she has designed a method for people, no matter where they are located, to experience the Toltec work and to build onto the teachings I originally presented in *The Four Agreements*.

Truly, if you engage in the methods suggested in this book, you will begin to change the dream of your life immediately. This work will allow you to identify the aspects of your belief system that are limiting the highest expression of yourself and to change a life of drama to a life of heaven on earth. All you have to do is allow Sheri to guide you into your heart and out of your mind, a mind which is filled with lies and fears. I encourage you to give her work a chance and just do your best!

With all my love & gratitude,
Don Miguel Ruiz

*There is a bit of controversy* regarding the origins of the common use of the word "spam" on the internet. Some feel it came from that crazy Monty Python song about Spam (the lunch meat). You might remember it went something like this:

> *"Spam spam spam spam.*
> *Lovely spam! Wonderful spam!*
> *Spam spa-a-a-a-am spam spa-a-a-a-am spam.*
> *Lovely spam! Lovely spam!*
> *Lovely spam! Lovely spam!*
> *Lovely spam!*
> *Spam spam spam spam...."*

— SPAM SONG BY MONTY PYTHON —

Either the word refers to these repetitious strings of verbiage that have no value of any kind, like in the song above, or it indeed refers to the lunch meat itself, which most of us don't want, don't care to eat, and certainly don't go out of our way to order.

Personally, I see the internal dialogue of the mind, that voice that is constantly chatting in our heads, as spam. It gossips all day long, telling us things that are not necessarily truth, and in fact are often self-limiting and self-sabotaging in nature. Mind spam is useless ongoing commentary which is neither wanted, needed, nor asked for.

It's like the endless flow of useless spam in our computer in-boxes, except that mind spam crowds out the important messages we need to focus our attention on, like the ones from our heart, integrity and Spirit.

This book is about obtaining freedom from spam and from the programming in our minds that is responsible for generating it!

# Preface

***More than ever,*** we're being exposed to alternative ways of living our lives. Self-help books tell us we can live in bliss and that the purpose of life is to be happy, yet at the end of the day, many of us can't imagine how that's possible in our own lives. "They" (these self-help books and the authors attached to them) are always talking about those other people, the ones who have more time, more money, less responsibilities, and more resources. We feel trapped by our lives and often resign ourselves to believing this is how it will be until we reach a certain age or a certain financial bracket — then we can be happy, then we can have fun.

*"The greatest discovery of my generation is that human beings can alter their lives by altering their attitudes of mind."*
— WILLIAM JAMES

An even more insidious trick of the mind tells us that we're already happy because we have absolutely no concept of what "real" happiness is. When I say real happiness, I mean the type of happiness that is not dependent on anything outside of ourselves, like our work, family, or financial status.  Most of us believe we're happy when things are going well in our lives, but if things took a turn for the worse and we lost everything, that happiness would be gone in a flash. If all the wonderful things and people in your life were taken away, would you still be able to say you were happy? I doubt it.

We've been domesticated to believe that we're at the mercy of life's circumstances. Our happiness and joy seem to be dependent on things that are occurring outside of us, events in our personal lives and world environment. We live life riding an emotional roller coaster, feeling happy one day and depressed, angry, frustrated, and jealous the next. We never consider that we have the ability to create our reality according to what we believe in our minds. No one has ever taught us that we can be happy all the time and that what happens out there does not have to take our happiness away. We don't have to feel victimized by our circumstances.

To be truly happy, we need to heal our emotional wounds and break the cycle of socialization that has held us captive to a particular mind set. I'm suggesting a way to do this based on simple common sense and an acute awareness of how the "program" in our domesticated mind works. By "program," I am referring to the totality of information and adopted beliefs contained within our rational minds as a result of our domestication and socialization. In essence, our programming is our own worst enemy, constantly telling us that we're not. It tells us that we're not beautiful or handsome enough, not strong enough, not clever enough, not smart enough, not brave enough, and not good enough. (And lest you think otherwise, realize that even the most successful people have these types of fears, self-loathing, and self-doubt.)

This type of internal dialogue is enough to make anyone unhappy, and truly qualifies as "mind spam." Our constant focus on what our minds are telling us keeps us locked into a limited point of view rather than on the infinite possibility of Spirit within us.

> *Obtaining true freedom (and by extension, true happiness) is what I am alluding to here, freedom from our own programming and mind spam, which means even a person incarcerated could become free from the beliefs that caused him or her to end up in jail in the first place. That example may seem extreme, but in essence, we all live in a jail of our own creation made up of the limitations we have imposed upon ourselves. The only way to change is to cultivate awareness of what we believe about ourselves and our world. Once we've taken stock of what's what, we can transform what is not serving us. After all, we can't change what we don't know exists!*

Over the years, I have observed with much sardonic humor how similar my mind is to that of my computer's. I started to see how everything that I do, think, and say is but a reflection of the totality of the program in my mind. I saw how all the major information necessary for my life in this reality was downloaded during my domestication, or childhood (something I'll go into greater detail about in Chapter 2). And the most fascinating thing I noticed was that not all of the contents of my program were necessarily true! There was information in there that was actually harmful to me and went against my integrity (meaning the oneness of the real spiritual me as part of the universal whole). I started to look at those harmful beliefs in my program as if they were viruses that were corrupting, distorting, and contaminating the way I saw and experienced the world. I realized I wasn't in charge of my life; instead, a program filled with virus-ridden beliefs and damaged files was! How could I have clarity regarding my life choices when I wasn't even making those choices for myself?

As anyone who has had contact with a computer knows, programs can be debugged, viruses quarantined, and corrupted files re-written. My goal is to make your process of transformation an enjoyable and fun experience, to assist you in the inventory of your program, and to search and seek out those aspects of your program that are stealing your happiness, joy, and emotional peace. You will also see that it's possible to reconcile the technical world in which you live with the spiritual being that you are.

# Section 1

## *The Mind's Program*

*"Neo, sooner or later you are going to realize just as I did,
there is a difference between knowing the path and walking the path."*

*— Morpheus, as said to Neo, "The Matrix"*

***The mind is a fascinating piece of machinery.*** We're taught at a very young age to think in certain ways, but we never acknowledge that the way we think isn't exactly the same as any other human! Although we've all been programmed with the same concepts and ideas, we haven't fully understood that we all have our own particular interpretation of what those concepts and ideas are. So even if we're speaking the same language, we have no idea if we actually comprehend each other in the way we intend to be comprehended!

It's no wonder that with all of the different programs interacting out there, our lives can get quite messy. This section will explain how we can begin to take charge of our own programming and thinking. The first step is in understanding it.

## *Life As A Program*

**Years ago I used to subscribe** to a soft covered book club, as I was an avid reader. In January 1998, I received a book written by author don Miguel Angel Ruiz (*The Four Agreements**), who was teaching Toltec philosophy and how to be happy in life. Well, you know the saying that when the student is ready, the teacher will come? As a result of receiving that book, don Miguel became my teacher and I the apprentice. It was the beginning of my journey of self-discovery (and a rocky one it was, I can assure you!). I was blessed to meet someone who has committed his life to reflecting to people that they are wonderful, deserving, and incredible manifestations of Spirit. He has the patience of a saint to devote so much time, energy, and love to help people see that they are incredibly beautiful, even though they argue against it to the very end.

So please let me share a little bit about myself with you and how I came to have a teacher in the first place. I grew up in Brooklyn and Staten Island, a feisty Jewish girl with a mischievous bent. After a "normal" childhood of public schools, Good Humor ice cream, malteds and summers on Coney Island Beach or in the Catskills, I escaped to the University of Buffalo for college. I say "escaped" because I grew up in your typical dysfunctional family and could not wait for the opportunity to leave home. An average teen, I had developed the same aspirations as my friends at the time. We were going to take advantage of the new opportunities available to us that our parents never had. And at the same time, we were going to get married and have families and great careers. After all, this was the '60s and '70s and we believed anything was possible.

My parents thought a good Jewish girl should become a doctor or a lawyer, so after college I entered Podiatry school. I received excellent grades and married a fellow I met during those medical school years. He was just what I thought I should marry. The "what"

*"Slow down baby, you're going too fast. You got your hands in the air with your feet on the gas. You're 'bout to wreck your future running from your past. You need to slow down baby, slow down baby."*

— *SLOW DOWN BY INDIA ARIE*

3

came from a list of requirements I had regarding what I believed would constitute the perfect mate. (For example, I believed that a man should come from a good family, be well-educated, be a hard worker, have the same religious beliefs as me, want children, and not drink or do drugs.) Of course my list of requirements reflected the programming my parents downloaded into my mind in my youth. He was a nice enough man, but I was not equipped with the skills needed to have a healthy relationship. Eventually we split up and I entered into serious relationship number two. I actually believed that if I picked a man opposite in personality to the first one that would solve my problems. Guess what? Marriage number two was headed for Doomsville!

Not only were my relationships not working, but I was overworked, tired, bored, stressed, and just not happy. (Sound familiar?) Having seemingly everything in life and being successful was not all it was cracked up to be! Yes, I experienced many happy moments over the years, but I realized I could not claim I was truly happy inside. It took approximately five years after the second marriage and an involvement in a new and painful relationship to see that I needed to do something. I was finally able to be honest enough to admit that I was neither happy with my life nor myself. After the demise of a third major relationship I realized I had to stop blaming everyone and everything else for my situation. The economy, the medical field, my parents, my husbands, the stock market, and society were not to blame for my state of affairs, I was. I had never been taught to take full responsibility for the life I had created for myself, at least not in the way my teacher eventually taught me to. I kept changing my life circumstances rather than addressing the real problem — myself.

By this time, I was experiencing heart palpitations and other stress-related symptoms — nothing incapacitating or debilitating, just a series of messages from my body telling me things were not going particularly well. I was tired of taking medications to keep each new set of "symptoms" at bay. Truly, I felt that if I didn't do something soon, I would die. What I didn't appreciate at the time was that I was dead already; I just didn't know it. So that was it. I had reached rock bottom. I couldn't live my life another day this way. I couldn't take another pill or have another painful relationship. So I did the only thing I could think of at the time: I put my podiatry practice in Florida up for sale, ditched my boyfriend, sold my townhouse, put everything into storage, and jumped in my car and left. I always had a flare for the dramatic.

That was just around the time I read don Miguel's book and decided to follow him around to his different lecture engagements and apprentice with him. I also used the time to travel about the West Coast of the U.S., hiking, relaxing, and meditating on my life. After a couple of years of serious self-reflection, quiet inner study, and much-needed brutal self-honesty, I moved to California to take up my studies more seriously and to work for don Miguel's organization. Many people who read his books don't realize they come from the Toltec tradition because they sound so much like plain old common sense.

Toltec philosophy is not a religion, although it contains the same basic teachings found in many esoteric and religious traditions. A more accurate description is that it's a way of living one's life that encourages alignment with one's integrity and Spirit. Toltec stresses things like learning to love yourself so that you can love others, and that we're all part of one being, so harming another will result in harming yourself. Ultimately you learn who you really are and that everything you need to be happy and successful in life is contained inside yourself and has always been.

You see that happiness can't be found outside you, no matter how far or how long you journey, nor is it something you can purchase with money or barter for with influence. No teacher can give happiness to you, nor can they wave a magic wand over your head and speed up your process. Finding true happiness takes absolute dedication to yourself and the path you are walking on, just like Dorothy's journey in *The Wizard of Oz*. She always had the ability to get herself back "home," but she needed to discover that for herself, to claim her own power, we can say. You too, can find your way back home, but you need to find the strength and personal power within yourself rather than hoping someone else will give it to you.

> *Please don't take these actions lightly! Growing up in a very pragmatic household made it difficult for me to just drop a successful medical practice in order to take off and follow some man from Mexico around the West Coast. My parents were convinced I had entered a cult; in fact, it's still a source of great humor for my family even now. My parents did eventually meet don Miguel and have been ever thankful for the wonderful influence his teachings have had on my life — and theirs.*

I must admit that my path of self-discovery and awareness was the most difficult thing I have ever involved myself in. Medical school was easy compared to delving into the deep dark corners of my own mind. I believed I was a focused, disciplined, intelligent person who could achieve any goal. What I didn't realize for many years is that although those are lovely traits to have, it's even more important to have patience, grace, gratitude, and love for ourselves in order to be able to make it past the denial system that guards the maze we call our mind. Honestly, these were kindnesses I never had learned to give myself! A good question to ask yourself at this point, with all the honesty in your heart, is if you have absolute patience, grace, gratitude, and unconditional love for yourself. The truth is most of us don't, and it's no wonder, since the importance of these skills are not emphasized in our society.

When I first started on the Toltec path I asked myself, "What do I want from these teachings?" I had read many of the popular published Toltec books, and they always talked about personal power and personal freedom. I figured that would be a good place to start, since the idea of personal freedom intrigued me. At the time I didn't truly understand what I was trying to break free from. The thought never entered my mind that I could be a prisoner of my own programming, domestication, and mind spam. I needed to understand for myself what constituted personal freedom and personal power.

My comprehension of those concepts has slowly evolved with time and experience. For me, personal power is all about freeing your faith from everything you believe about yourself and your world. You have personal energy invested in maintaining, justifying, and protecting the things you believe in and that particular energy constitutes your faith or your personal power. To put it plainly, if you let go of everything you were taught to believe to be true and right in your life, all the faith you had invested in those beliefs would return back to you. The benefit of this type of process is that you can re-deploy all that personal power and energy into making the changes in your life you've always wanted to make.

*Perhaps you have seen the movie "The Matrix." Neo, our hero, spends the entire movie learning that he has been living his life putting his faith blindly into an interactive computer program for his mind. But by the end of the picture, he has taken his faith and personal power out of the program and redirected it into believing in himself and life. With that faith in himself, he is capable of performing great miracles. Yes, this is only a movie, but the concepts are absolutely applicable in our lives. We, too, are all capable of great miracles if we have faith in ourselves instead of our programming. These are very powerful concepts and I will talk more about them throughout this book.*

During my years of traveling this path, I've looked for less esoteric and more practical methods of expressing these concepts. I've always felt that these teachings would be so much more accessible to people if they could be put in terms that we use in our everyday lives. As I became more involved in the Toltec path, I was able to see how much my mind behaves just like the computer on my desk, which has no freedom to behave any differently than it was programmed to. To alleviate my tendency to get dramatic and despondent, I made the choice to find a way to make it funny. To that end, and to help you understand all of this more clearly, I will use computer analogies throughout the rest of this book.

# *The Program And Its Pitfalls*

***Picture the brain*** as the most amazing computer ever created. Not only is it capable of orchestrating the mind to create a perfect 3-D virtual reality of the world we live in, but it can also perform calculations and memorize huge amounts of information. If that's not enough, the mind is also capable of filtering and interpreting the incoming perceptions that our human bodies react emotionally to.

*"The most merciful thing in the world, I think, is the inability of the human mind to correlate all its contents."*
— *H.P. LOVECRAFT*

Imagine that when a child is born, it has a brand new Pentium IV hard drive, but with no software included in the package. At this point, the baby's "computer" interacts through its capacity to react emotionally. It feels Mommy's warm body and it smiles and coos. When it's tired or it poops, it cries. It doesn't have any information in its program yet to explain or understand what it's experiencing, it just experiences! Unless a baby is sick, tired, hungry, or has just relieved itself in its diaper, it's happy and full of love.

From the time a child is very small, the humans around him or her start downloading millions upon millions of bytes of information and spam into the little computer. Parents start by teaching language, words for people and objects like "mommy," "daddy," "bottle," and "cookie." Later, as a child matures, parents start teaching abstract concepts — for example: love, family, friendship, ugly, pretty, stupid, smart, right and wrong, and what constitutes a good child versus a bad one. In teaching these concepts, parents domesticate their child by downloading files pertaining to social rules that exist in our reality and by using reward and punishment. If a child is a "good" boy or girl, he or she will get a reward and parental love. If the child does not obey the program, he or she will be punished. This training helps reinforce the socialization files so that no harm comes to the new little computer out in the world.

In the beginning, most of what comprises a child's computer program has been given to them from their parents, an entire set of human concept files and their corresponding beliefs. As the child becomes older, though, information and spam starts coming in from sources other than their parents, and all of the downloaded files are not compatible. Parents, friends, family, TV, school, books, magazines, radio, and religious education teachers all download different information files into the child, in addition to all of the child's personal experiences and encounters. Amazingly, the mind actually finds a way to make some kind of sense of all this incoming information and files it in a way that makes it accessible at a moment's notice. It creates an actual structure for all the incoming data, like a massive filing cabinet.

Every time we acquire a new belief in our program, we have to agree with it in order for it to be accepted by the mind's computer, sort of like clicking on the "I accept" button when you are installing new software on our home computers. For example, if your parents told you that God lives in the sky and watches over us, you accepted that belief and it became part of your religion file. If they told you that you are ugly or stupid, that belief was put in your self-worth file.

> *How do we fall prey to this domestication process? Simply because we believe our parents. As children we don't know any better. Even if a child asks, "Why, Mommy?" parents keep repeating their own beliefs until the child agrees and accepts those beliefs as truth.*

Once we grow up, we actually don't need our parents to domesticate and socialize us anymore because we have their belief system, programming, and spam imbedded in our mind. Think about the voice in your own head. Can't you just hear your parents talking? That voice tells you, "No, you can't do that. Yes, you can do this. That would be appropriate, but this would be inappropriate." Even if your parents are no longer living, you may still be arguing with them in your mind! That voice in your head originates from stored information in your computer program. In other words, every stored file has the capacity to open and display its contents to you at any moment, sort of like those unwanted pop-up advertisements that appear on the screen of your computer when you're on-line. It's a constant barrage of extraneous information, or what I call mind spam.

We go through life experiencing everything through the eyes of our program. We perceive and interact with our reality depending on the information we already have stored in our computer, in addition to the daily accumulation of our personal experiences, which supports what we already believe. Once a belief is added to the program by agreement, a piece of personal power goes along with it to secure the file in place. As I said earlier, your personal power is your faith that the piece of information you just agreed to accept and download into your program is absolute truth. Once you put your faith into a belief, it becomes yours to keep. By the time you are an adult, you have accumulated thousands of concept files filled with multitudes of varying beliefs!

Many of these files have corrupt information, though. For example, if you were told as a child that you were not lovable and you believed it, that belief in your self-esteem file will act like a virus, corrupting and damaging many other files and creating the capacity for the computer to crash at any moment. (After all, if your home computer had executive or system files that were not totally compatible with one another or had corrupt information, do you think it could process information correctly? Absolutely not!)

This means every time you engage in a relationship, the "I am not lovable" belief in your self-esteem file will be opened and it will contaminate your perception and experience of the relationship. Moreover, your program will make sure that you create situations in life that prove and support the contents of your files. In this case, that means you will continue to have relationships that constantly prove to you that you are not lovable until you decide that you are not going to put your faith or personal power into that belief anymore! I think you can see how our beliefs color our experiences, and not always for the higher good.

> *We go though life experiencing everything through the eyes of our program. We perceive and interact with our reality depending on the information we've already stored in our computer, in addition to the daily accumulation of personal experiences, which support what we already believe to be true.*

It's the brain's job to take the sum of all the information the senses receive, and filter it though the information and experiences already contained in the mind's program files. The mind will then analyze, pigeon-hole, define, index, sort, label, register, log in, classify, catalog, compartmentalize, and categorize every situation it encounters! Ultimately these files affect our ability to make healthy and wise choices in our lives. As a result, we don't have clarity in our lives simply because we're always interpreting our situations through these conflicting and corrupt files.

Even more fascinating is that, by the time we're adults, we actually come to believe we're our computer program! In other words, we think "we" are the ones who are thinking. We totally forget that "we" are the entity we call "Spirit" that lives between the cells of our own body and we're not our mind or the totality of our programming. "We," as Spirit, have the power to utilize the program's files or not. Do you see how insidious the belief system and domestication are?

- Imagine if you had the ability to review the entirety of your system files and reorganize and re-structure your entire program.

- Imagine if you could rewrite all your corrupt and damaged files and quarantine all the viruses.

- Imagine if you could transform all your files that tell you that you are not wonderful, smart, beautiful, handsome, fun, creative, successful, friendly and loving.

- Imagine if you could re-program yourself to believe you are capable of a most wonderful life filled with joy, happiness and love.

I'm here to tell you that you can do all of this. You are not required to hold onto beliefs that are creating unhappiness in your life! Now, that's what I call personal power!

You need your personal power to be intact in order to change the circumstances and conditions in your life. If your personal power is totally invested in maintaining your program, in what you believe about yourself and what you can or can't accomplish in life, nothing will change. Only by changing what you believe can you change your life. Failure to recognize this as a first step is the reason why so many people have read tons of books or taken classes and workshops and still find no real change in their lives.

The problem is our personal power and faith is all tied up maintaining a contaminated program. Our faith is the magic power that Spirit has endowed all of us with. Another word for this is Intent (In Toltec terms), which is our power of creation, the force that life uses to manifest itself in this reality. But instead of creating wonder and beauty in life, we spend every ounce of energy defending and supporting our beliefs, most of them based in fear. Using our awareness, we can choose which beliefs are borne of love and are serving us, and which spring from fear and are limiting our lives.

A limiting, fear-based belief that I found in my own program (dating back to my childhood), is that a person must be in a relationship to be complete in life, fulfilled and happy. This belief is based in the fear that a person isn't capable of making it on their own and that they have no self-worth without a partner. After all, if you can't get a partner, something must be wrong with you and you could end up a "spinster." Thankfully, I no longer subscribe to that belief but there are still millions of people who believe they will never survive without a partner, that they aren't good enough, not smart enough, not educated enough, or not innovative enough to make it on their own. They feel like failures without a relationship, rejected and alone. That's why so many people stay in relationships with partners that are abusive or just plain unrewarding rather than going solo. It's also why internet dating services are so popular.

If your own self-worth file contains a belief that says you are stupid and can never accomplish certain things in life, your life will be a very limited, self-fulfilling prophesy. Thy will be done. If you believe you are shy or ugly, what do you think life will reflect to you? If your faith is invested in these virus-ridden beliefs, your program and the universe will make sure your beliefs will be proven to be true. This is how Intent works. What you believe is what manifests in your life.

> *The concept that what you believe is what you create in life is not a new one, and can be found in many traditions including Christianity, Judaism, and Buddhism. Look at this example from the New Testament, John 1:1: "In the beginning there was the Word, and the Word was with God and the Word was God." What we believe is what exits our mouth, and what exits our mouth, our word, is the power invested in us by Spirit to create our reality. When we use our word in vain, by speaking badly about ourselves or others, what are we doing with that gift of word? Are we creating a life of happiness, peace, and love?*

The first time the structure of your program was created, you accepted all those concepts and beliefs without question, but as an adult, you have the ability to open the file cabinet, look through your files again, and decide which ones are no longer serving you. If you look carefully, you can see that there is no inherent reality to any information in your program. Beliefs are quite arbitrary. Facts can be changed or manipulated. Truth depends on your personal point of view, the century you live in, or the country where you reside. (Knowing this, we have to ask ourselves why humans argue with loved ones, go to war, and waste their precious time and energy defending what is not even real.) By doing an inventory of the mind, the files that are not working can be transferred into a special storage cabinet reserved for items that are no longer useful. This allows you to create a new reality using your free will and to exercise choice as to which beliefs you'll invest your faith in.

Since humans are creatures of habit, we can easily look at our lives and see the patterns that have consistently repeated themselves. (An excellent example of this is the pattern I shared with you in Chapter 1 regarding the multiple unhealthy relationships in my own life.) Basically, we're always reacting to situations rather than taking action in them. Why? Because we have no free will available. Free will means having the ability to make a choice. With all of our faith tied up in supporting and maintaining the beliefs in our program, we're left with very little personal power to make choices outside of the box. If I keep acting the same way in my relationships, is it any wonder that they always turn out the same way?

In any given situation, someone may say or do something that will "push your buttons." Immediately, without even thinking, you go into reaction. You can't even stop yourself; it's as if you're on auto-pilot. Even if you know you're about to say or do something you'll later regret, you can't stop; it's as if you are possessed. Indeed, you are possessed by the computer program in your mind. A specific type of event will trigger very specific emotional responses, behaviors, and actions based on events that occurred during your domestication period and the beliefs and agreements you made regarding those events.

For example, perhaps your mother has always been demanding and prone to laying guilt trips on you. When she calls and says; "Why don't you ever call me or come over for dinner?" you feel an argument welling up within you. Immediately, you go into reaction as your mind spam tells you, "I need to defend myself against her accusations." This is because you have a belief deep in your program that says you are a bad child, and you can never please your parents. Of course your mother can't make you feel guilty unless you already feel that you are. The guilt comes from the belief that you should please your parents and do everything that they tell you to do to be loved and approved of.

Perhaps when your partner forgets to take the garbage out, your reactions are caused by a different set of old beliefs than what sets you off where your mother is concerned. Maybe your partner has never been much help around the house, or he always waits for you to blow up before he'll lift a finger. As a result, chores have become a battle ground. When you come home from working all day and see the smelly garbage in the kitchen, you go into reaction, becoming emotional and engaging in the same old unhealthy behavior patterns: "He hasn't completed his chores as a considerate partner should. I don't feel appreciated because my partner is not doing things the way I know they should be done, and I am sure as heck going to let him know about it. Doesn't my partner know what his responsibilities are (according to my point of view)?"

As in the example with your mother, there's no free will available to behave in a different way, only reactions, a series of behaviors based on wanting to be right according to the point of view of your programming and your past experiences. Click on a certain type of situation and a particular outcome plays out. It was quite a realization for me to see that I never acted in my life, only reacted based on my programming.

> *Normally, beliefs evolve slowly with time, but even if you have adopted new and more supportive beliefs, I'll bet many of your old virus-contaminated and corrupt beliefs are still driving your life, working insidiously behind the scenes. They act as hidden executive or system files that you can't easily find in your program. That is why you do things that you later regret and why you can't stop yourself from saying things and behaving in ways that you know are not healthy for you, physically or emotionally. For example, you don't want to argue with your mother, but somehow you do it anyway.*

As humans, we only have a certain amount of energy per day. How we choose to use that allotment is up to us. You know how exhausted you feel after an argument? Well, imagine that you have used your allotment of energy for the day in that quarrel. Sometimes, we're even exhausted the following day because not only have we used that day's energy allotment but we've borrowed energy from the subsequent day! Now, after wearing yourself out in this way, do you really feel like changing things in your life? Probably not!

We waste our personal power and energy when we argue with other people about what we think is right, or about the way something should be done. Truth is relative and changes with your point of view. Imagine a big beach ball with pictures of several animals scattered around its perimeter. If you were looking at one side of the ball you might see a bear. If I were standing opposite you, I might be seeing a lion. Both of us would insist the ball contained only what we could visualize, a bear for you, and a lion for me. We would both be expressing what we believe about the ball from our personal points of view. Although both of us would see a portion of the truth about the ball, neither of us would have the whole truth, which can only be seen when you take into account all possible points of view.

When you think you're right about something and are ready to defend yourself, think carefully if you have truly considered all possible points of view or if you're operating from the limited perspective of your personal beliefs. We frivolously use our power by arguing, getting angry, defensive, jealous, and by holding grudges — all because we have to be right and because we don't recognize that we're just defending a belief in a program — and one that isn't necessarily truth!

As a result, if you spend your day defending and justifying your point of view and what you believe about yourself, you won't have any free energy to change what you don't like in your life. (Turning on the TV or watching a movie to zone out is sometimes all you have the strength to do after engaging in some particularly unpleasant interactions.) It will seem that your life remains the same year after year. If you defend your belief that you can't get out of your current circumstances because you don't have the money, you have children to take care of, no one cares about you, you can't leave your current relationship, you have too much work and not enough time, etc., surely nothing will change in your life. All your energy and personal power will go into supporting your belief that you are stuck and a victim of your circumstances. This doesn't have to be the case, though.

*These are the steps needed to reprogram and eliminate our mind spam:*

- First, take inventory of the totality of the program and all the beliefs and spam contained within its files.

- Second, quarantine and sequester all infecting viruses and isolate the files they have corrupted.

- Third, heal the damage the viruses created in your program so it can function and run in a healthy way so you can cease your reactive behaviors and emotional responses. To do this you must re-write and replace all the virus-ridden beliefs contained within your damaged and corrupted system files.

- Last, add files that are specifically designed to create and support love and happiness and optimize the efficiency and speed of the program.

By following these four steps you will be on your way to a happier and better functioning mind — which is exactly what we will be doing in this book!

# Chapter 3

# *The Universe In The Mind*

*In Chapter 2, I talked about* how the program is formed, how information is downloaded into the mind, and how we use our faith to hold those beliefs in place. Now we need to look at how what we perceive with the senses affects the creation of the program. This is critical because everything we perceive and experience in life is received by the brain and either affects or is affected by the mind's program. To be able to understand this process I'm going to explain how the brain receives information and how that information is processed and perceived. And no, you don't have to be a doctor to understand this; it's actually very simple.

Your eyes are open. You see a book before you, correct? Well, how are you seeing? You're seeing because there is light present. Light hits objects and people, bouncing off them all the time. This light goes in through your pupil and lens, and creates a little image on your retina, the special tissue which is located in the back of your eye. Then your optic nerve (the big nerve that collects all the information that has been recorded on your retina) transforms all this information into a series of chemical and electrical messages. These messages then split off and spread along multiple nerves taking the picture of this book into many sections of your brain. Based on this information, you can say you have never seen an object in your whole life, just the patterns of light reflecting off of those objects. In other words, your brain assembles the object in your mind for you to "see," a true virtual reality! There the information is interpreted, analyzed, qualified, and pigeon-holed.

Your eyes function just like mirrors since they contain a tiny replica of the outside reality projected onto the back of your eyes. Therefore, no interpretation is done in the eye at all. Once the brain receives the information, it sends it to various areas to be processed. This same procedure occurs with your other four senses too, although

*"Few are those who see with their own eyes and feel with their own hearts."*

— *ALBERT EINSTEIN*

sight and hearing tend to dominate. The brain creates a 3-D image in the virtual reality of your mind of the person or object you are observing and interprets and analyzes the information according to what you have been taught and what you have experienced. This is normal, and is exactly what the brain is supposed to do. Two scenarios can occur any time you perceive: Your perception is either filtered through the multitude of program files and distorted or colored by what you already believe; or the perception is new and creates a belief or agreement in the program based on what you are experiencing for the first time.

For instance, let's say as a child, you had an uncomfortable experience with a brown-haired girl from Brooklyn. Maybe she was a bully who used to beat you up. As an adult, your friend introduces you to a woman with brown hair who has a Brooklyn accent. Your retina receives this picture and then sends it to your brain. Then your mind says, "Oooh, I don't like her. I know what she's about." Or perhaps instead your best friend from Brooklyn had brown hair and your childhood world revolved around her. In this case, you entered information into your friendship file as a child and made an agreement that brown-haired Brooklyn girls are great. As a result, upon meeting a brown-haired Brooklynite as an adult, your mind interprets the data according to your past and you hear, "Oh, that woman looks very sweet. I would like to know her personally." In both cases, you have perceived this new woman with your senses, but interpreted and reacted to her according to what you have experienced in the past. What you believe in your program about brown-haired Brooklyn gals has colored your current life experience. This happens subconsciously, as it's part of our computer's function.

If you grew up in a home where your family always talked derisively about people of other religions or races, you would have put that information in your file on humanity and you would take this information as truth. As you matured, you would experience everything through these beliefs and they would color your perception of everyone you meet in life. Your agreements would affect whom you choose as a friend, who you work for, date, or marry. Since you would interpret everything through your program, all of your experiences in life would only confirm what you already believe. In other words, your beliefs would help to create situations confirming that people of different races or color should not be trusted or even associated with. Until you consciously decided to take your faith out of those fear-based beliefs, they would continue to act as viruses, infecting all of your interpersonal relationships. Perhaps these beliefs would prevent you from having a wonderful relationship with a person of another color or race just because of what you were taught as a child.

> *Have you ever talked with a friend about something that happened years ago and you wonder if the two of you were actually present at the same event? He tells you the whole story about what he remembers, you tell him the whole story about what you remember, and then you just look at each other in disbelief! Then each one of you starts trying to convince the other that your version of what happened is the correct one. Now you understand why this type of situation occurs — although you have both witnessed a single event, your past experiences personalize your individual interpretations of that event.*

Let's look at a more involved example of the above. Imagine that you grew up in a home where you were always yelled at and your parents were always arguing with one another. The situation was so bad that you had to go live with a relative where no one in that family gave you love and you had to fend for yourself. As a result of your little mind's interpretation of your childhood experiences, you adopted a belief that you are not lovable or wanted. With your faith and personal power, you put that belief in the self-worth file of your program. As an adult, none of your relationships have worked. With time, you have come to see that you created all those failed relationships and situations to prove your childhood beliefs to be true.

With recapitulation (the act of reviewing your past), it becomes obvious to you that you have always been very cold in relationships and afraid to let anyone through your defenses. Every time someone got too close to you, you behaved in a way that drove that person out of your life. You see that you have been overly argumentative (just like your parents were) and that you've had a need for everyone to prove to you that they loved you. Yet you sabotaged their love with your icy attitude. The people in your life simply got tired of your behavior and left. This may seem like an extreme example, but in actuality it's a very common one. Take some time to think about this scenario and whether it contains anything that applies to you.

I think we can clearly see how our program is affected by our perception, previously downloaded files, and past experiences. There's a whole universe that exists in our mind that no one else shares. This is why communication between people can be difficult. We all perceive the exact same things but don't interpret them the same way. But for whatever reason, we assume everyone understands and knows what we have in our head. It seems odd when we look at it this way, doesn't it? That's why things are not always what we think they are and why our truth is only relative. It's also why people do and say things that don't seem to make sense to us. How can we know the beliefs that drive other people to do the things they do when we don't even fully understand why we do the things we do or what our own beliefs are?

The bottom line is that we all have fear-based beliefs in our programming and they create unhappiness and suffering in our lives because they don't serve our higher good. They act as viruses contaminating how we perceive and experience our world. If we can identify all these beliefs in our own mind, we can change them and the way we perceive ourselves and the world.

# Chapter 4

## *Values And Concepts Become Corrupted*

*We're all so busy* and immersed in our own lives that we're totally unaware of the lies we all are living. Think about this for a moment: From the time you were young, you were taught how to be a man or a woman, what it means to be a man or a woman, what men and women do, and where they can go in life. But — according to whom? According to your parents, your teachers, the TV, and the movies? According to this society, the big program out there? Does anything that you have been taught have any inherent truth to it? What if this life, this reality, were something totally different? You never had a chance to choose your reality; you were born into it, and of course, you bought the illusion, lock, stock, and barrel.

Many times along my path I have asked myself, who am I really? Growing up in the '60s and '70s it was considered cool to ask those types of "metaphysical" questions. I was 40 years old when I realized I still was asking the same questions, living the same stressful life, and didn't know one iota more about who I was than I had when I was young! So much for the belief about being older and wiser! In reality I was more stubborn, opinionated, and rigid. At that point, it became a crisis of sorts to truly understand who I was. I asked myself, am I just a compilation of my experiences on this planet, a combination of all I have been taught or am I the formless, limitless woman that Spirit has placed in this manifest form we call the body? Am I really what I believe I am? Am I my personality? Are you?

When you say, "This is how I like to dress, this is the music I like, the car I drive, the neighborhood I live in, the furniture I have," who is really saying that? Is it the computer program in your mind, what you have been taught to believe, or is it the real you? Is it really true that you have to look the way you do, speak the way you do, or choose the friends you have? Are you really the religion you were born into, the color of your skin, or the profession you work in? Do

"It's the customary fate of new truths to begin as heresies and to end as superstitions."

— THOMAS HENRY HUXLEY

25

you call yourself ugly, short, tall, skinny, fat, stupid, smart, funny, serious, shy, outgoing, poor, or rich? Are you truly any of those things? Have you ever considered the limitations you have put on the expression of your Spirit by the way you describe yourself?

> *When I was practicing medicine, I was a fan of jazz and classical music. Upon looking at my beliefs on a deeper level, I came to realize I believed that "intelligent people" listened to these types of music, and I wanted people to see how educated and sophisticated I was, so I convinced myself that I loved these genres of music. The truth is that I love many types of music: R&B, rap, pop, rock & roll, and world music in addition to jazz and classical. I was limiting my experience of what I was willing to listen to because I didn't want to be judged for listening to "lesser" music. To be able to admit something like this to yourself takes the ability to be absolutely truthful and fearless regarding the contents of your program. If we have thousands of beliefs like this that limit our enjoyment of life, how can we be truly happy and free to express ourselves? Without awareness, I would never have moved past my denial system to be able to see this limiting belief.*

Humans have values and concepts in our program that other living beings on earth don't. We have concepts like marriage, relationships, money, work, vacation, property, health, fashion, war, religion, sports, education, manners, food, politics, friendship, family, etc. Every person you meet has opinions and beliefs on each concept based on their own program. Let's look at a very practical example of this: Imagine you have been married for several years and your anniversary is coming up. In your mind, you believe that if your partner loves you, he will surprise you with a lovely gift or even a night out on the town. Instead, the big day comes and you receive a blender. Now you're really angry. You start an argument with your beloved, saying, "You don't care enough about me to put some real thought into what I would like for a gift. We've been together all these years and all you can think to buy me is a blender? You probably forgot about our anniversary and got this at the last minute. If you really loved me, you would have bought me something nice! You are the worst and most inconsiderate partner!"

What would have to be in your programming in order for this argument to occur? First, there's the concept of marriage and all of its inherent rules. Obviously, there is a belief that one must celebrate the anniversary of a marriage. Then there is the belief that there is great importance in recognizing that date. There is a file about what constitutes a proper gift. The cost and the quality are important and there are rules about what items can even qualify as a gift, and not only qualify as a gift, but as a gift for this particular occasion. Then there are rules from the love files which state in a nutshell, that if your mate loves you, he should know exactly what you have in your program. He should have the ability to figure out exactly what makes you happy by anticipating your every need (which is exactly what he would have done if he knew the contents of your programming).

In the above example, you would have used what you believe about marriage and love and twisted and distorted it to justify and defend what you believe your partner should do for you. You would then feel justified to argue and be angry with your partner for what you feel are his shortcomings. Your partner's program, on the other hand, may tell him that anniversaries are not important and that living a happy life together is all that matters. To him, a blender may be the perfect gift for entertaining. He probably never thought this type of reaction would the result from this gift. This is a perfect example of how we hurt others by defending what we have in our programs.

*It's also possible to take the concept of friendship and manipulate friends into doing a favor for you by saying, "If you were my friend, you would help me move. After all, I always help you out when you need it." Who said friendship means having to do what you ask of someone? Or you can manipulate and distort the concept of honesty by saying, "Oh, I am not stealing those things from work. They have plenty of money and they don't pay me what I deserve anyway." Any concept can be twisted to reflect warped programming.*

If we look carefully at our beliefs, we can see all the trouble they can create in our lives and our world. When we believe in things that are coming from fear, happiness can't possibly be the result. An extreme example of this would be the tragic events of 9/11. When Osama Bin Laden orchestrated the bombing of the World Trade Center, he did so because his beliefs regard Americans as evil, unclean infidels and that his actions would be rewarded by Allah. Many people were very angry at the Moslem faith and the Moslem people because of this. But it's neither the religion nor the Moslem people who are at fault; after all, the Moslem faith teaches love. One man took the beautiful writings of the Koran and the Moslem faith and twisted and distorted them because of the viruses contained in his personal program.

Once the teachings were corrupted in his own mind, he felt justified taking action according to what he believed. If our personal beliefs are based in fear — fear of people different from us, fear of different religions, political systems, race or color — only anger, hatred and violence can result. In return, our fear of people who we believe are not like us, justifies our actions in waging war on them. Fear-based beliefs begetting more fear-based beliefs. Believing we're all separate (the concept of duality) rather than part of the One is the root of this fear.

At one point in time, I believed that there was evil in the world, but I don't believe that at all anymore. I feel that people are all manifestations of Spirit and that evil is a result of the presence of corrupted virus-ridden files in the minds of human beings and people obeying the contents of those files. When we take knowledge and distort it and believe things that aren't true, it creates fear in human beings. It's then that they are capable of committing indescribable acts of violence and evil.

Of course, our actions may not be as devastatingly violent as Bin Laden's, but we definitely have hurt our friends and family with our need to be right. We justify and defend our beliefs and make them correct at the expense of others. We all take these wonderful human concepts and twist and distort them to support our personal point of view. How many people in your life have suffered as a result of your defending your own fear-based beliefs? Take some time right now to think of how you do this in your life.

# Silencing Spam With Spirit

**Your programs files and beliefs** have been spamming you constantly as you have been reading this book. While trying to understanding the many new concepts here, you may be having a conversation in your head that sounds like, "Oh, that's interesting. I wonder what she means by that?" or, "Hmm, I don't like what she just said." As I mentioned earlier, your mind is just doing its job of qualifying and analyzing everything it perceives and comparing it to what is already contained within your program. Understanding this is important because it's essential to be able to recognize the difference between the real you, or Spirit, and your program. If you can't tell the difference between your mind and your Spirit, you will always be tempted to listen to your spam (which sometimes can be quite tasty but not necessarily good for you).

Simply put, Spirit speaks through the heart with your feelings and not through your mind with words. Oftentimes, you will hear something in your head and think it's Spirit speaking but this is not truth. Spirit's silent and is easily hidden by the noisy mind and its programming. The mind likes to be boss; it's very smart and certainly does not want to relinquish its power to Spirit, which is the expression of your heart. It's constantly talking to (or spamming) you, to divert your attention from your heart. When the program in your mind stops you from trusting your gut feelings or intuition, this is what is happening! By recognizing and acknowledging this process, you can start listening to your true self instead of a program filled with false information.

The real self is "no-thing," as opposed to nothing. Spirit has no name, personality, race, color, or body type. Many, perhaps most, people relate very strongly with the belief that they are the color of their skin or their race, but only the physical body has these attributes. When we die, of course, we don't take our physical body

*"And now here is my secret, a very simple secret; it's only with the heart that one can see rightly, what is essential to the eye."*

— ANTOINE DE SAINT-EXUPERY

31

with us. Although I grew up Caucasian and Jewish, I now realize that I am truly neither one of these things. Caucasian is just what color we attribute to skin like mine — and color in itself is a just a human concept.

> *Not all creatures on earth even perceive color! For example, my mother's dog can't tell the difference between a Caucasian, an Oriental, or an African-American person. She only sees black and white and shades of grey! Bats see with sonar and have no eyesight at all. All humans look the same to them.*

Religion is another human concept, something we have invented in response to a calling we feel deep inside us. But Spirit can't be defined by the dogma humans have created with their religious practices. Spirit is simply "I am." It exists, it's conscious, it's aware, it creates, it's life, and it's unconditional love. Even using the word "Spirit" and my lovely descriptions are limiting the expression of that which is "no-thing."

At the beginning of my journey, I found it difficult to realize that I was not my mind or my body — after all, I am thinking and moving, aren't I? Our association with ourselves as Spirit rather than as mind or body (or matter) is certainly a complex concept to ponder! The way I was able to understand this better was with a little experimental mind game. Imagine for a moment that you had one leg amputated. Would you still consider yourself "you" if one part of your body was missing? What if you had both legs removed — would you still be you? What if both legs, both arms, and all your non-essential organs were removed — then what?

All matter, ourselves included, is made of atoms. They compose our skin, hair, eyes, brain, cells, organs, blood, etc. So then what resides in between the millions of atoms composing our body? You do! As Spirit, you are present in your physical body, living in between and around the atoms that your body is composed of. That is why when a body part is physically removed, "we" are still there, whole and undisturbed. Your Spirit can't be cut off from you or split into parts or pieces.

To express yourself on this plane of reality, you must use the vehicle you have been given, your body. Luckily for all of us, this vehicle includes one great computer, the mind. But we're not the computer; we only utilize it. Once I could picture this, I was able to start separating myself from my mind. I understood that my mind had a program and I could choose to use the program or not, or change the program as needed. I stopped believing the mind spam and fear-based things my mind was telling me. It was easier for me to see how arbitrary the beliefs in my mind were. I started to connect with a vague feeling of unconditional love, peace and contentment I had deep within me. Later, I was not only able to expand this feeling of divine consciousness within me, but I was able to connect with the divine presence within all living things.

It's important to understand that anyone can have this kind of experience with Spirit but in order to do so, one must detach totally from the mind. In fact, most humans have actually experienced this at some time but never really understood what transpired. For example, have you ever had your breath taken away from you just by perceiving the beauty and immensity of nature? You know the kind of feeling that is so overwhelming it brings tears to your eyes and takes your breath away? You're not thinking in those moments, just perceiving with all your senses and feeling. Why do you think you're having this kind of emotional reaction? Well, it's quite simple; you're perceiving the real you reflected within the immensity of nature, your true self, the absolute wonder of the perfection of creation, and the unconditional expression of universal love.

Imagine if all humans had this awareness. No one would bother to go to war over religion or any other invented human concept because they would realize that there is only the illusion of difference. No one would bother to attach their self-worth to their body weight, clothing brands, car, or where they live! People would not try to impose their beliefs on others because they would know they are arbitrary. It's possible to live in a world like this, but we all need to come to feel that this is true for ourselves and not just because we read it in a book. I can assure you that once you have an actual experience as Spirit, this will no longer just be a theosophical theory. And the more you separate yourself from the noisy voices and mind spam in your head, the more you will feel Spirit moving through you. With time, you may even be able to quiet your inner dialogue and totally detach from it. You don't need that spam talking in your head 24/7 in order to survive in the world — even though your mind would have you believing that you do!

# Section 2

## *Taking Inventory Of Your Program's Files*

*"Most people think that shadows follow, precede or surround beings or objects. The truth is that they also surround words, ideas, desires, deeds, impulses and memories."*

— *ELIE WIESEL*

***Now that we know how the mind works,*** we can start looking deeper into what's really in there. What do we believe, and why? Are there truly any "right" or "wrong" beliefs or just different ways of seeing the same exact thing? We often hurt ourselves with our beliefs without ever realizing what we're doing! In addition, we also reflect what we believe about ourselves — our core beliefs — onto others, which leads to all sorts of judgmental interactions.

In this section, we'll start picking apart and taking an inventory of the belief system as we prepare to dismantle the program behind it.

## *Letting Go Of Judgments And Beliefs*

**Let's get down to business** and start looking at what's in your computer. Taking an inventory of your files will give you the knowledge of which beliefs are not serving you and what needs to be changed. Reading this book may give you this awareness, but putting it into practice in your life is integral to your success. That part is up to you, and is what we'll be discussing in this chapter.

An inventory is simply an accounting of all the beliefs and concepts you have within your programmed mind. Every belief of what you think is right or wrong, or good or bad is part of this inventory. Anything that you can conceptualize or debate is part of your inventory. It's the totality of everything you can think about in your mind. In my experience, the most effective method of taking inventory of your program is by writing down all your beliefs in a journal — in other words, by downloading your program onto paper.

For the most part, it's not a simple task to sit down and just write everything you believe about everything; after all, if you already knew what you believed, there would be no need for this type of self-evaluation! We're all constantly judging, whether or not we express these judgments out loud for others to hear. Once you can visualize your judgments on paper, you can examine the beliefs lurking behind them and work to dismantle them.

It's helpful to have a good understanding of how judgments, opinions, and beliefs are related prior to beginning this inventory. A judgment is an assertion of something you believe. A belief is simply your acceptance or trust that a statement, concept, or tenet is true or valid. You have to believe in something to be able to pass a judgment. For example, if I believe that my bed-sheets should be changed weekly, then I will judge people who don't change their

*"Judge not, that ye be not judged. For with what judgment ye judge, ye shall be judged: and with what measure ye mete, it shall be measured to you again."*
— ST. MATTHEW 7:1-2

sheets weekly to be dirty and gross. If I believe that people should date a person ten times before making love to them then I will judge those who sleep with people on the first date to be "loose." Or suppose I believe that people should not be chatty, that they should only say what they need to say. Then I will judge talkative people to be annoying and irritating.

It's damaging enough to our human relationships when we judge others according to our personal beliefs. Engaging our beliefs for self-abuse and using our judgment against ourselves is even more detrimental. So, for example, if I didn't get a chance to wash the sheets this week, it will bother me and I will be uncomfortable and feel gross until I do. If I slept with someone on the second date, I will feel regret and anger toward myself for my irresponsible behavior. And if I find myself talking more than usual with someone whose company I enjoy, I may chastise myself later for behaving foolishly. A common question people ask is, "Are all of my opinions judgments?" This is a great question to address. Let's define these concepts:

*Opinion: A belief or conclusion held with confidence, but not substantiated by positive knowledge or proof.*

*Judgment: The capacity to form an opinion by distinguishing and evaluating based on one's beliefs.*

Opinions and judgments originate from information contained within your belief system. You can only make a judgment by evaluating and distinguishing based on what you believe. However, if what you believe is not necessarily the truth, not only is the judgment without value, but any opinion you come to as a result of that errant judgment is not necessarily truth either! If all of your beliefs are rather arbitrary, then so are your opinions and judgments. If, as a doctor, I say you should not eat eggs because your cholesterol is high, that is my opinion, based in my belief that eggs are high in cholesterol, which may lead to a heart attack. This, in turn, is based on a belief in the medical community that there is an absolute correlation between eggs, cholesterol, and heart attacks. However, medical beliefs are time-sensitive, and since I first learned about this correlation, we have found that people on high-protein diets — which include eggs — don't necessarily develop high cholesterol all the time. And in twenty years, who knows what we will believe, not just about eggs and cholesterol but about anything! Which beliefs are truth, what is opinion, and where is the absolute proof?

Next, it's important to understand the difference between discrimination and judgment. There are times when it's necessary to discriminate, or to make a distinction between certain things. For example, you're in a restaurant and must decide between the lamb chops and the vegetable dish. This decision will either be based on your own personal preferences or by engaging your judgment to make the choice. If you say, "I feel like lamb tonight rather than veggies," this is your personal preference. It isn't as if you are saying that lamb is better or worse than vegetables. This is discrimination between the two, not a judgment for or against. But, if you say that eating meat is terrible because we shouldn't kill animals, you are stating an opinion and making a judgment. Why? Because you have a food file containing a belief that eating animals is not appropriate. But — according to whom? This is just a belief in which there is no inherent truth. In other words, this is "not substantiated by positive knowledge or proof."

> *You are not respecting other people's beliefs when you impose your viewpoint on them or try to get them to change what they accept as truth. It's up to them to inventory their own program and decide for themselves if a particular belief is worth changing. Spirit has given every human the gift of choice. (Remember free will?) It's up to each individual to decide how to use it.*

Sometimes a situation in life requires an opinion, such as when your opinion is requested at work. Given your experience and the information that you currently have in your program, your opinion could be helpful to others. But you know now that other opinions are as valid as yours, and that you can only express your personal point of view on any given subject. Knowing this makes it easier to be detached from your opinions and the need to be right, therefore making it easier to hear others' points of views and to arrive at solutions with ease rather than by argument. In this way, multiple human computer programs can share their information, or "network," rather than having to defend and justify the contents of their files. This allows the general program of our society at large to grow and progress by peaceful exchange of ideas and concepts rather than evolving through disagreement or war.

As humans, we hold a very special gift from Spirit: the ability to create concepts. Over thousands and thousands of years, we have given birth to millions of concepts. Once these concepts are conceived, we formulate our own rules appropriate to each concept. The ability to create concepts and beliefs and then use our rules about them to pass judgment on others is what creates most of our suffering as humans. We forget that our concepts and beliefs are subjective. We disregard our personal responsibility for the beliefs we have created and forget to have respect for what others believe. When we take what we believe and torture ourselves and others with it, or when we use these very concepts to imprison ourselves, we're demonstrating a total lack of awareness regarding what's in our own mind.

Imagine you're sitting in the mall having a coffee, just watching people walk by. It's interesting to watch the amount of judgments and spam generated by the beliefs that are contained within your program. If you see a woman in a short skirt and think to yourself, "How can that woman leave the house dressed like that?" You obviously have beliefs about how women should be dressed, yourself included. Maybe this woman is fifty years old and she is dressing like she is twenty, and according to your program, a woman her age should dress more conservatively. Or maybe you feel her skirt is too short and she looks trashy. You might believe that she's too heavy, according to your program, and that her clothes are too tight. Perhaps she's wearing white and it's after Labor Day. The list of potential judgments goes on and on.

> *The most important thing to realize is the way you judge others is the way you judge yourself. If you have concerns about being overweight, for example, you may be limiting the way you express yourself with clothes, all because of the fashion rules you have been taught according to TV, your mom, or fashion magazines, and the limiting beliefs you have about your own physical body and self-worth. It may not seem like these thoughts are causing you any harm, but if you constantly torture yourself with diets and exercise or by telling yourself you are fat or ugly, these beliefs and judgments are not serving your happiness.*

Let's say you see some teenagers from your seat in the mall and think, "I would never let my kids leave the house in those baggy clothes and I certainly would not let any kid of mine smoke!" Perhaps your program is telling you that parents who allow their children to wear baggy clothes are neglectful or that these parents have no control over their kids. (After all, they allowed the child to leave the house in the morning dressed like that, didn't they?) Also, you might think that any parent worth their salt would smell cigarette smoke on their child and stop that behavior immediately. You might say to yourself, "Doesn't that child have parents who wash their clothes and smell the smoke? Obviously these parents don't care." Can you see all the beliefs and judgments represented here? Think of how often you make comments like these to others or to yourself in your own head.

We define ourselves by what others think about us, by their opinions and judgments. This is something we have been taught to do since we were children, and a state of mind that our society encourages constantly. For example, we make judging what everyone is wearing to the Emmys and Oscars a national pastime! This judging perpetuates the need to "look appropriate" according to what the fashion industry dictates and encourages us to constantly measure ourselves and our self-worth against the opinions and beliefs of others.

But think how empowered you would feel if you never cared about what anyone thought of you and you could express yourself exactly as your heart wished. Imagine how great it would be not to be under the constraints of other people's judgments, opinions, and beliefs, or how nice it would be to feel that you don't need your family and friends' opinions or advice to do anything in your life. To reach this point, you need to be able to get out from under your own beliefs first. Remember the quote about judgments from the New Testament at the opening of this chapter? Ending your judging is about ending suffering, fear, and pain and creating a world filled with love and happiness.

For myself, I don't think any happiness or love comes from the way we judge, nor do I feel that humans are in the position to be judging anything. The trees don't judge the earth, dogs and cats don't judge their masters, and the grass does not judge the rain or the sun. The universe is what it is, and we don't have the bigger picture of why things are this way. If we did, perhaps we could find meaning in the many things that confuse and befuddle us as humans. The truth is that we don't have this information and there are some things that we can never know from the point of view of our reason. Awareness of this can facilitate the end of our criticizing and judging so we can just accept life on life's terms, especially when we see that all the information in our program is rather subjective.

### *Action list to identify concepts, opinions and judgments:*

- Can you list ten human concepts in addition to the ones listed above in this chapter?

- Can you identify five times today that you freely gave your opinion without the other person asking you for one?

- Why did you give those opinions? Look carefully at how you justified your answer to my last question.

- Now ask yourself honestly if your justification was just a reflection of your self-importance, the need to make yourself right, and the need to feel good about yourself.

- Can you identify five times you made a judgment today?

- What beliefs were those judgments based on?

- Was there really any truth to your judgments?

# *From Simple To Core Beliefs*

**Before we can effectively inventory our beliefs,** we need to consider what we have beliefs about. As we discussed earlier, we have beliefs regarding all of our human concepts. Let's make a list of a few of those concepts. We have food, decorating, home, fashion, music, art, happiness, friendship, family, politics, money, property, cooking, religion, education, gifting, relationships, marriage, justice, economics, wealth, abundance, fun, strength, community, passion, spirituality, creativity, fame, service, charity, competition, humor, beauty, talent, evolution, science, service, kindness, intelligence, courage, wisdom, purity, righteousness, retirement, and work. I could list thousands upon thousands of concepts here and we have hundreds of beliefs about each one, so in no way is this list comprehensive. I am sure you can think of many others too, like sports, parenting, vacations, war, etc.

Our beliefs run the gamut from being simple and relatively insignificant in nature to those that contain very complex values that go to the very core of our being. The need to defend our simplest beliefs often causes the most trouble in our lives. For example, in the very beginning of my Toltec studies, I was working with a wonderful teacher named Gini, and I was staying at her lovely casa in Santa Fe for the purpose of obtaining help with dismantling my belief system. One day, as I was preparing my grandmother's recipe for chicken soup, Gini said, "Why don't you put those chicken livers in your soup?" I said, "I would be happy to grill the livers for the dog, but I will not put them in my soup." I explained that the livers are dirty and they don't belong in the soup. Gini was adamant about me putting those livers in the soup! I got really angry and said, "Under no circumstances will I put those livers in there! That's not how a person makes chicken soup!"

After a few minutes of conflict and getting myself aggravated, Gini told me, "Sheri, the purpose of my request is to push you to see what

*"What you have become is the price you paid to get what you used to want."*
— MIGNON MC LAUGHLIN

you believe about chicken soup so that you can see the nonsense that you have your personal power invested in." I never realized how many rules I had in my program about chicken soup. I saw my beliefs about which parts of the chicken I considered clean, about washing and boiling the chicken in a certain way, about cutting the carrots one way and the onions another, about tossing some dill into the soup — and I could go on.

Well, the livers never did go in the soup that day, but I did come to realize that I was wasting my personal power and energy defending and justifying my point of view about soup. My Italian girlfriend makes her chicken soup one way and my Greek friend makes hers another way. Don Miguel's family is from Mexico and they put avocado and corn in their chicken soup. Are any of us owners of the one true way of making chicken soup? Sure, this example may seem like silliness, but I suggest that you make a list of the ways you defend your point of view about the rules you have in your program regarding other concepts, both major and minor. In the above situation, I gave my happiness away to Gini, wasted my personal energy by arguing with her, and raised my blood pressure to boot. How many times in a day do you do the same thing? It's the minor beliefs like these that are the cause of most of the daily conflict in our lives and the source of the multitude of resentments we harbor against people we love.

Here is another example of a simple belief. I was traveling with my teacher, assisting him at a lecture, when he stopped by my room to take me to the venue. He saw one of those pillows that helps keep your neck in alignment on my bed. He said "Oooo, I like that pillow. So many of these hotel pillows are uncomfortable and my neck aches. That looks like it would be really comfortable." I thought to myself that I would get him one for his birthday. Some months later, on another trip, he spied the pillow again. He said, "I wish I had a pillow like that." I told him he was in luck because I was going to get him one for his birthday, which was two months away. He said

"Sheri, I want the pillow now. I need it now." I could not imagine anyone being so rude, inconsiderate, and impolite, demanding his birthday present like that. I told him he could have his pillow on his birthday. Again, he asked me for the pillow right then.

We went back and forth a few times like this until I was frustrated and angry. Finally, he said "Sheri, I have no intention of arguing with you over anything. The reason I said this is to make you look at what you believe about gifting. If you needed a winter coat in December and I knew it, why should I wait until your birthday in April to give it to you? Why does a birthday present need to be given on that day? I suggest you make a list of the rules you have in your program about gifting. Also, I recommend you look at your judgment against me because of what you believe and how you were ready to fight me over a pillow." And so I did, and I bought him the pillow as soon as I got back home!

Perhaps you find that you believe it's disgusting to have dirty dishes sitting in the sink all day long. You may have been raised to believe a clean kitchen is imperative and that you are a bad homemaker if you leave the house with dirty dishes in the sink. You may worry that people could drop by and judge you to be a dirty person. And remember, we always judge others as we judge ourselves, so you may visit the homes of others and say to yourself or to a friend, "Gosh, Mary's kitchen is a mess. There's stuff piled up in the sink and all over the counters and the place looks greasy to me. I don't even feel like eating here. If my place looked like this, I certainly wouldn't be having company over."

Consider this: If you can't get out of the house in the morning without cleaning everything up first, and because of this, by the time you do leave the house, you are tired and stressed, that's an abuse of your body. The belief that you can't leave the house messy causes this abuse. If you are being controlled by your beliefs and you can't go against your own rules, that is a sure sign of trouble.

So let's say you decide to leave the house messy in the morning. If you are thinking about the house all day long, or if the minute you get home, the first thing you do is start cleaning, you are attached to and controlled by your beliefs. In creating a beautiful and happy life, we need to tell ourselves the truth about what we believe and whether those beliefs are really bringing us joy.

This is how it is with all of us. We're not aware we have programmed beliefs; we just think we're right! Well, the rules we have about any subject are subjective. They are not the absolute truth. We don't have to believe anything we have in the program. My suggestion is for you to question everything you believe about everything. The good thing about these simple beliefs is that we don't have a lot of energy or personal power invested into them, so usually, once we're aware of their presence, we can change them if we so desire.

As a result of my own awareness, I decided that I did not have to make chicken soup in any particular way, nor was it necessary to be so particular about gifting. I just made a list of all my beliefs on those subjects and then rewrote them to thoughts that expressed love. So now my food file contains a belief about chicken soup that reads like this: "My grandmother's chicken soup is made a particular way, but all versions of chicken soup are equally acceptable, as are any ingredients. There are no limits on the expression of chicken soup in my life." My gifting beliefs read as such: "A gift can be given at any time, regardless of the occasion. From now on it's strictly an expression of my love for others and I only gift when I want to and not because I have to. Gifts are now my pleasure and not my obligation." If you re-write those beliefs about the dishes in the sink from the homemaking file, they might look like this: "I enjoy a clean and neat home, but I no longer let that desire stop me from enjoying my life. I know I am a wonderful person and I don't care what others think about me or how they might judge my ability to keep my house. I no longer link my self-worth to what others believe about me and the cleanliness of my home." See? That wasn't too difficult!

Now let's talk about beliefs that are more intermediate in complexity. Don Miguel had just finished giving a beautiful dissertation on the belief system at one of the lecture venues I was assisting him with. At the break, a lovely lady came up to me and said, "You have the best job." You get to travel all over with a speaker and get to work with such wonderful people. It's marvelous." I asked, "Is this something that you would like to do?" She said, "I would love to, but I can't." When I asked why, she replied, "Oh I'm shy. I could never do that."

I said, "You just listened to don Miguel speaking for an hour and a half on the belief system and the limitations that it causes and look what just came out of your mouth! You just put that limitation on yourself and by doing so, you eliminated an entire career from your life because you believe you're shy. Isn't that amazing? We do that every day and we don't even have the awareness that we're doing it. What you utter from your mouth is what you manifest in your life." Once she had that awareness, she said, "Oh my gosh! I can't believe I said that. Now I realize what I've been doing." Because of her new awareness, she has the power to make a choice whether she wants to get over her shyness and walk through her fear.

Fears can be conquered and beliefs broken. I promise you there is no fear or belief that you can't get over if your desire and intent is strong. And yes, sometimes we need help. On my first spiritual journey, to the ruins of Teotihuacán (outside of Mexico City), my teacher told us that we were going to climb the Pyramid of the Sun. I had a morbid fear of heights with vertigo, nausea, the whole thing. I figured I would try to climb a smaller pyramid, the Pyramid of the Moon, for practice. I went up that pyramid step by step on my booty until I got to the first level. I was dripping with sweat and shaking! I said, "This is it. There is no way I'm going to make it to the top of this pyramid, so how am I going to make it up the larger one?"

I went to my teacher and told him how I had tried to conquer my fear of heights without success. He said, "I will help you." He spent a little time with me and my fear-based beliefs and then told me to go join my group to depart for the pyramid. I started feeling very emotional. I went part way up the pyramid and froze. Five beautiful women who were also on the journey came around me with all the love in their hearts and helped me to the top of the pyramid. Of course, if I had not really been ready to confront my fear, they never would have been able to get me to move. When I got to the top, my teacher hung me off the side of the pyramid by my feet! I tell you, it was quite an experience! My belief about heights has now been changed to read, "I love having the vantage point of an eagle. It's a blessing to have such a clear and expanded point of view. I enjoy all my life experiences to the fullest and don't fear death, from heights or otherwise."

> *To ask for help is difficult for those of us who have a belief that we should be able to do for ourselves and that asking for help is a sign of weakness. I was one of those people who never asked for help. I always had to do it myself. I recognized it came from a belief my grandmother gave me growing up: "God helps those who help themselves." I've come to realize that sometimes we all need a little help and it doesn't mean we're wimpy! Since then I have rewritten the belief that I don't need help to say, "All people have been gifted by Spirit with expertise that I can benefit from if I ask. I welcome with joy and gratitude any help that can make my life more beautiful and easy."*

The most effective way of changing beliefs and behaviors is by behaving in a different way from how you would normally operate. You can call your normal habitual behaviors your "doings" — these are the ways that you traditionally conduct yourself in any given situation. Therefore, when you do something differently than usual, you can say it's a "not-doing." This works for changing simple, intermediate, and core beliefs. (My climbing the Pyramid of the Sun was a definite not-doing for me, while leaving the house "dirty" might be a challenging not-doing for you!)

Now, let's look at an example of what I call core beliefs, something that all humans have. These beliefs are like dark shadows lying behind the images we project to others. These take more detective work to locate and also require strength and courage to admit to yourself that this is what you really believe.

When I was young, I was called "the walking talking stick ball bat with the rat trap in her mouth." As you can imagine, I was very hurt by this teasing. I believed the other kids were right; I was a skinny geek. I compensated for that lie by adjusting my personality to become an entertaining and humorous person. Over the years, this became second nature to me and I described myself as a fun girl to be around. Toltecs call this the "mask" that we create to cover over the lies that we believe about ourselves. My lies were that I was ugly and not good enough the way I was. As I got older, my mask became more refined and complex. My teacher used to purposely call me "Dr. Rosenthal" in the early years of my Toltec training because that name represented the most dominant aspects of my personality, those which formed my main mask. It was the way that, as an adult, I protected myself from the world so that no one would know that deep down, I was still "the walking talking stickball bat with a rat trap in her mouth."

"Dr. Rosenthal" had it all together; she was very smart and articulate and you couldn't argue with her because she was always right. You would never have known that a skinny, nerdy little girl with glasses and braces was living inside her, holding onto that mask, trying to protect herself. (Sometimes a mask alone is not effective enough to hide our lies so we do things like take drugs, drink, or otherwise numb the mind just so that we don't have to see what's underneath the mask.) The projected image or personality of "Dr. Rosenthal" was not real and neither was the little girl who was "the walking talking stickball bat with the rat trap in her mouth." Both were absolute lies. The truth is that we're all magnificent human beings, all beautiful and wonderful, but we don't believe that because our self-worth files have been contaminated with these corrupted beliefs and the masks we have created to cover over the whole mess.

> *You can see that the denial system is the most fantastic protective mechanism we have. It will do its best to make life bearable. My denial system created a way to cover over my hurts and wounds so neither I nor other people could see how I really felt about myself. We do this all the time but we don't see ourselves doing it. The system is quite flawless and ingenious and works perfectly without our awareness. I would have sworn to you that "funny" was how I was, that it was part of my personality. But we're not our personality. As you can see, we create our personality in reaction to our experiences in life. I could have easily gone the other direction and become quiet and just said I am a shy person. That would have covered over my discomfort and insecurity just as effectively.*

Let's say you grew up in a home where there was a lot of violence. Your father beat you and your siblings regularly, but as a child you could not understand the reasons why. Perhaps your parents yelled at you and told you that you were useless and ugly and that you would never amount to anything. As a result, you grew up ashamed of your home and your family and believed that it was normal for the people you love to hurt you. You saw that violence was an expression of love and accepted it as customary.

As an adult, you always ended up in relationships where you and your partner screamed at each other and emotional abuse was a daily affair. Maybe your partner hit you, or perhaps you were the one doing the hitting. Of course you didn't like it, but none of this was out of the ordinary, and despite the physical abuse, you believed your partner loved you. It was the only way he or she knew how to express what they believed was love, and violence was all you knew love could be. These kinds of beliefs — that you don't deserve love, that the people you love hurt you, that you don't deserve any better in life, that yelling and verbal abuse is normal, that you hate yourself and are ashamed of yourself — are core beliefs. We have a lot of our personal power invested in them.

Looking within ourselves for these beliefs it is not an easy task, because we dig up things that hurt us so many years ago. You might be asking, "Why is it necessary to dredge up all that old stuff that doesn't even matter anymore?" It does matter, because each of those core beliefs contains the viruses that have contaminated your program. Even though those events happened years ago, your program runs according to those agreements and beliefs you made when you originally downloaded that spam into your program.

In my case, I agreed that I was skinny and ugly and that the other kids were correct to tease me. Once that virus entered my program, it infected all my self-esteem files and changed the way I saw myself. From that moment on, I became uncomfortable with my physical appearance. I dressed to hide my thinness, became funny to hide my ugliness, and avoided situations that put me in the public eye. As an adult I felt uncomfortable wearing a bathing suit or "sexy" clothing, or getting naked with men. (I wanted to wear sexy things to attract a guy, but then once I had him I didn't want to be naked in the light.)

All of these beliefs and agreements create the emotional reactions and behaviors that play out later in our lives. Who as an adult thinks to themselves, "Gee, I must feel this way because of the wounding I had when I was eleven years old?" No, the mind with its efficient denial system will cover that neatly by saying, "Oh, I hate being in a bathing suit because I need to lose five pounds and do some serious exercise. Once I lose that weight, I will be fine." Except you never lose the weight because you need it to protect yourself, see? If you lost the weight, you would have to admit to yourself that you hate yourself regardless of the weight. So absolutely, those events from long ago affect everything we do and everything we are right now in this very moment.

Let's list some of those core beliefs that may be hiding in your program. You can work at finding any that I have not listed here!

- The people who love you will hurt you.
- You will never be as good as your siblings or others.
- You can't trust anyone.
- Life is suffering and pain.
- You will never have financial security in life.
- You can never do anything right.
- You are trash, garbage, or worthless.
- You are geeky, nerdy, and uncoordinated physically.
- You are not an intelligent person or a good student.
- You will never have a good job or successful business.
- You are ugly, fat, thin, gross, disgusting; your body is not **normal**.
- You will never have love in your life; you are not lovable.
- You hate yourself; you wish you were someone else.
- You never know when you will lose everything you have, or when everything will be taken from you.
- Everyone who loves you leaves you.
- You are invisible and worthless.
- You are nothing without the approval of others.
- If you are perfect then you will be lovable.
- You are so ashamed of yourself; you are a terrible person.
- Life is filled with injustice.
- No one cares about you; no one will save you or come to your defense.
- You can never be forgiven for your sins.
- You can never have abundance.
- No one ever listens to you.
- You don't deserve anything better in life.
- You don't deserve respect from others.

The first step in the process of creating an inventory is finding the truth and having awareness about what has really happened in your life and the beliefs that you have about yourself as a result. That means looking at your life from a neutral position, and seeing your life truthfully, not how you want to see it, and most certainly not from the position of a victim.

You may be saying to yourself, "Oh, this is not my situation. I am successful in life. I have a good business and marriage. I'm happy and I didn't grow up in an unhappy home or unhealthy situation." Regardless of your humble or not-so-humble beginnings, you may still have core virus-ridden beliefs that are preventing the unlimited expression of yourself. It's very possible that you just haven't been honest enough with yourself to see them. It's not necessary to have grown up in a violent and abusive home to have judgment against yourself. No matter how apparently successful you are in life, you can still use your word against yourself and others and whether you realize it or not, those words will manifest in your life one way or another.

Inventory your program with honesty. Once this is completed, you can identify the viruses contained within the program. All viruses must then be quarantined (something we'll discuss in Section 3) and the files that they have damaged, rewritten. So in my case, once I identified the virus created by my childhood experience, I was able to see how it created distortion of my life from that point on. I could only perceive my life through that virus. Once I was able to quarantine the virus, I took that lie and rewrote it to say, "I am beautiful and lovely just the way I am. Spirit gave me a long, lithe body in this lifetime and I adore it." The next step was to forgive myself for believing that lie for so many years. It's also a good idea to forgive the person or people who gave us these viruses) in the first place. The action of forgiveness allows us to detach from the lies, and this is what constitutes the quarantine process.

> *When you've spent your whole life believing certain things and practicing behaviors that go against yourself, it takes a lot of courage to change. It's like learning to play an instrument; it takes lots of practice. In this case, practice doesn't make perfect; instead, practice creates mastery. Mastering self-love and happiness is a full-time activity and you are the only one who can initiate that action.*

Many folks use their word to manifest unhealthy relationships and life situations with people who are more than happy to prove to them that what they believe about themselves is truth. This is why some people end up in the same kinds of situations over and over again. To stop that cycle, we need to stop believing the lies that work against ourselves. This is not easy when you believe in your programming that you are no good or undeserving of respect. We can rewrite these files to read, "I love myself and will never allow myself to be abused by anyone, even myself. I am a wonderful person with lots of love to share. I understand other peoples' pain and forgive them for abusing me. Furthermore, I forgive myself for allowing it."

Because so much personal power and faith is invested in these types of core beliefs, simply being aware of them is not enough to change them. Only action will make a difference. And by action, I mean that the only way to change these beliefs is to create situations that prove to yourself that you are lovable, kind, and smart. It starts by looking at the contents of your self-esteem files with honesty and changing the way you treat yourself. Once you start treating yourself with respect and loving yourself unconditionally just the way you are, then other people will treat you the same way.

> *You can only create what you feel you deserve in life. You have to be willing to leave any relationship or situation that goes against you, realizing that you don't need those kinds of dramas because you choose to love yourself 100 percent. It helps to engage a healthy person in your life to help you with this, so that when you are feeling weak, you don't go back to your old ways. Instead, let the other person assist you in staying strong and not believing your self-defeating mind spam.*

It's imperative that your beliefs be at your service so that you can engage them whenever you like for your happiness rather than being enslaved by your beliefs where they are abusing you and making you suffer. The mind should be at the service of the heart and not the other way around. Remember, you are not your mind; you have the ability to engage it at anytime, but you don't have to believe the voices and spam in your head. There is an old Jewish proverb that says, "The devil comes to us in our hour of darkness, but we don't have to let him in. And we don't have to listen either." Good advice!

We're always focused on the internal dialogue, or mind spam, being generated by our programming. We hear that nonsense in our head all the time and believe it. When you hear those voices in your head, determine what they are saying, but don't believe them or listen to them if they are trying to hurt you or create limitation in your life. They're just infected program files wanting your attention like the pop-up ads opening on your computer. By not giving my attention to the mind spam in my head and by rewriting my corrupt files, I was able to totally transform the program in my mind to a pleasant and loving environment.

### *Action list for identifying our self-limiting beliefs:*

- Can you identify five simple beliefs that you defended today as truth? In other words, can you identify some of your "rules" that you feel are absolutely right and that you imposed on another person or yourself?

- Can you identify five judgments you made today that went against yourself? What did you hear your mind telling you in each situation?

- Can you name five things you believe about yourself that you know are preventing you from accomplishing more in your life?

- Can you name five core beliefs that you have about yourself which you realize are harmful to yourself?

- Have you previously tried letting go of these beliefs and judgments? Were you successful? If you were not — why weren't you?

## *Initiating The Virus Scan*

***Once you start to download*** your judgments and beliefs on paper you can figure for yourself which beliefs are working for you and which ones are not. As you work through those program files keep your eyes open for those that have been corrupted and have brought unhappiness and limitation to your life. This is the actual process of initiating the virus scan. Don't try to make this happen overnight because you'll become frustrated and angry. It took me years to totally evaluate my programming and let go of all the associated anger, resentment, pain and damaging beliefs that I insisted on hanging on to. Have patience with yourself; this isn't a contest and there's no finish line.

Let's look at some common beliefs that we have about different human concepts so that you can have a better understanding of this process. This first list concerns what people believe about work. Ask yourself how many of these apply to you:

- Work is too competitive and unsatisfying.
- Work comes first, play second.
- Work is good because we need it to keep our minds active.
- If you enjoy your work, the money will come.
- Work is a means to an end and is necessary whether you enjoy it or not.
- You have to earn a living by doing what makes money and not necessarily what you enjoy.
- Work is part of your personal growth and development.
- You have to work in order to live and pay your bills.
- Work should involve a marketable skill that you can do forever.
- You can't work too hard.
- There is no difficult work, just work to be done.
- The early bird gets the worm.
- Work is about honor and commitment.

*"People often say that this or that person has not yet found himself. But the self is not something that one finds. It's something that one creates."*
— THOMAS SZASZ

- Work reflects your passion.
- It's a system of rewards and punishment.
- Work is challenging and satisfying.
- It's an affirmative means of creating joy and fulfillment in life.
- Work is a means of serving others.
- We need to work in order to be good human beings.
- Men should get paid more than women since they must support the family.
- Women have to work harder than men to get raises and good pay.
- Woman should be paid less because they are not serious about their careers and may leave to have children.
- Your career is what you do for the rest of your life, so you'd better choose it carefully.
- Work is play, an expression of creativity and joy.
- You define yourself by what you do.
- Idle hands are the devil's workshop.

When I was growing up, I was taught you had to work very hard if you wanted to become something, and if you were a woman, I was told, you had to work even harder because you had to prove yourself. In my family, a woman could be a doctor or lawyer or get a Masters or Ph.D. in business. Why? It was important to have a skill that was marketable, so that you never had to depend on a man for your income. A doctor was a good choice because everyone gets sick whether there is a recession or not, and I would always have a job. Because my parents experienced World War II, a steady income was considered an important matter. Of course, this is just a point of view according to a particular time frame and my family's personal beliefs. But if I put my faith in these beliefs, I will manifest my life only from this particular point of view, which is quite limiting.

If you found yourself agreeing with what my family said, that is because you have those same beliefs in your programming. Your program was aligning with mine; this is how we make ourselves right. If someone agrees with me, I can believe that what I am saying is correct. This is how we perpetuate beliefs that are not necessarily truth.

Remember: Question whether your beliefs are bringing you joy and happiness. If I have a belief that says that I have to work harder than a man to make it, then I have to work sixty hours a week instead of forty. That belief is going to have consequences in my life and I have to make a decision whether I'm living my life or my beliefs are living my life for me. It's challenging to change our beliefs because they are habitual and we've been practicing them for years. I started practicing the Toltec work when I was forty years old. Imagine forty years of doing the same thing over and over again! I didn't have the strength to change a lot of the things that I wanted to change. And most importantly, I didn't have awareness about the things I really needed to change.

Of course, work is far from the only concept that we have strong feelings about. For example, how do we really feel about husbands and fathers? Read the following list and check off your beliefs:

- A father must support the family.
- A man must be strong and not show when he is worried.
- He is responsible for all the major family decisions.
- A man should be in charge of the money.
- A man needs to take care of his wife, please her, and make her happy.
- A father must spend time on the weekend with the kids.
- Fathers are disciplinarians; hugging and kissing the kids is the mom's job.
- A father should be affectionate and loving.
- A man should not let his wife work and certainly should not be a "mister mom."

- Men should know how to fix things in the home, since they are in charge of maintenance.
- It's okay to be a single father.
- A single father needs to get a wife to take care of his children.
- Fathers lay down the law in the home.

Now let's look at some beliefs we have about what a wife and mother should be:

- A mother is the glue that holds the family together.
- She should be a problem solver and good at organizing and coordinating a lot of things at the same time.
- She should be gentle, loving, nurturing, generous, harmonious, inspiring to her children, and a good listener.
- A mother should be ladylike, feminine, and gentle but strong.
- She should be the caretaker, the nurturer, and a breadwinner.
- She should have children, keep a clean a home, and not work.
- A mother should be a pillar of strength.
- She should be loving and kind and devoted to her children without letting life get in the way.
- Women should want to be mothers.
- A wife should let the man think he is smarter than she is.
- A woman should take good care of her husband, never raise her voice, remain calm, be a good example and love the children.
- A woman should always look good, not be aggressive, and satisfy her husband sexually.
- A mother should be able to work outside the home and have a career or stay at home if she wants to.
- A wife and mother should be in charge of the house and its entire doings.
- She should be a good cook and make things everyone likes.
- She must know how to help the kids with their homework and be supportive of their after school activities.
- Mothers can be single if they want to and don't need a husband.

As we look at these lists of beliefs, we can clearly see that many of them are conflicting. These represent the voices of the many beliefs in our heads, whether we currently think we have our faith invested in them or not. For example, if you are a woman, you may remember your grandmother saying, "You have to please your husband, you have to be a good wife, and you have to be a good mother." Perhaps when you were older, you started reading articles in magazines that said women and men should be equal, that we can be sexually aggressive, that we don't have to be mothers. Well, those beliefs would be in your head too. All of these beliefs exist simultaneously in the program of your mind. How are you supposed to be happy or make choices when your mind is filled with conflicting information?

Now that you are getting the idea here, let's delve a little deeper and look at another set of beliefs that we deal with every day. We all have to eat to survive, but we all have different ideas about what that means to us.

Beliefs we have about food:

- Food is comforting; it relieves stress, anxiety and uncomfortable feelings.
- Food makes you fat and causes you shame.
- The food you eat should be healthy.
- You must take supplements because your food is not healthy.
- Salad is rabbit food.
- You eat to live; you don't really like food.
- You live to eat; you derive pleasure from food.
- You can't handle the temptation of food.
- People should not eat meat because of the terrible chemicals used in its production and because of the way the animals are treated.
- Food is something you experience socially, for fun and entertainment.

- You can't control your life, but you can control what you eat.
- Food is love.
- You have to eat all of your food because other people are starving.
- You can manipulate people with food.
- You can use food to abuse yourself and to hide behind.
- You should not eat candy, chocolate, deserts, or other bad foods.
- You must eat a balanced diet or you are not eating properly.
- The burping and farting resulting from eating is disgusting.

What we believe about food and eating is such a loaded topic. We've been taught so many different conflicting things about food: how to eat it, how to cook and prepare it, its importance and value both socially and physically. We use food to manipulate people, to gain control over them and to barter with. It took me quite a while to decipher all the beliefs I had on this subject. For example, why do we feel guilty if we have chocolate or something else we "shouldn't" eat? Who decided which things are bad for us to eat and which things are OK? Why should children eat everything on their plates? Why is it rude to slurp soup in the U.S. but it's a compliment in other countries? Why is it bad to eat with your left hand in many counties and not in the U.S.? Why are cows sacred in some places and eaten in others? Why do some people keep kosher and other people abstain from alcohol? Why do some people eat food and then purposely throw it up? Why do people use food to hurt others or themselves?

There are also many different customs and ways of interacting with food. In and of themselves, most food rituals are lovely expressions of the different human traditions and religions around the world. If we understood that this diversity was the result of local food availabilities and preservation techniques, along with local traditions designed to promote survival, it would be great, but mostly these concepts we have about food are now used to create separation between people. (For example, cultures that were nomadic often dried their animal meats so that they would travel without rotting.) We're responsible for the creation of these human concepts and traditions, but we forget there is no right or wrong. This is what happens when we become attached to what we believe and need to make it right at the cost of making another wrong.

The other side of this coin is how we use these concepts against ourselves. While growing up, we learn so many things about food and body image. We use food to control, punish, and manipulate ourselves. When we're upset, we use food for comfort because we don't have the self-love available to give to ourselves. We want to look a certain way to be accepted by society, so we control the food that we eat and in that way, attach our self-worth to what others think about us. We deny our enjoyment of food so that we can punish ourselves. We make food our enemy, as if it's sabotaging our existence. By investigating the underlying beliefs behind these behaviors, we can clearly see why we're engaging in harmful activities.

Since we have the opportunity to re-write our beliefs about food (or about any concept for that matter), once we look deeply at those beliefs, we can also look at changing the way we experience food. Changing your beliefs directly affects how you perceive and experience life, so this is an important part of the process. As a little experiment, imagine that you have gratitude and respect for your food while eating it rather than just eating it without thought. Try viewing your food as something that gave up its life so that you could go on existing. It doesn't matter if it's a head of lettuce or a slice of cow; neither entity is living anymore. Imagine having respect for those living beings that sacrificed themselves for you. Imagine that you are absorbing the energy of that being so that you can fuel your metabolism. And in having absolute respect and gratitude for your food, try eating with all of your attention on it. Rather than reading the paper or a book or looking at TV when eating (you have no idea what you are eating or how much!), focus all your attention on how the food tastes. Enjoy your food and the sensual experience that food can be. Notice how grapes burst in your mouth, chocolate slowly melts, apples are tart and crunchy fried chicken is juicy and yummy. Your experience of food will totally change as a result of this exercise.

Now let's look at some beliefs that are harmful to us and limit our ability to be happy and to have love-filled lives. I have included just a few categories and in no way are these lists inclusive. If you think of some beliefs that are not on these lists, please feel free to add them in and personalize them. As we go along, check off all the beliefs that you have in your program. Let's see how many of these beliefs you'd be willing to argue for, even if they're fear-based. Please note that some of these beliefs are gender-specific, while others apply to both males and females.

Beliefs we use against ourselves to hurt our bodies:

- It's necessary to be thin to succeed; even if one must use laxatives or vomit not to gain weight, it's worth it.
- You must exercise until you look perfect.
- As soon as you age, you are going to have plastic surgery — you don't plan on looking old.
- It's okay for a man to get old, but not a woman.
- You need plastic surgery to make your body look more balanced aesthetically.
- You need to look fashionable/hot/sexy to get attention.
- You are not good looking and it's not likely you will find a mate, so you might as well eat what you want.
- Cigarettes/drugs/alcohol/partying won't hurt you; you're just having fun since you work hard and deserve to enjoy yourself.
- You are spiritually aware and since you don't believe that cigarettes or alcohol can hurt you, they won't.

Beliefs we hurt ourselves with in our relationships:

- Women should defer to their partner in a relationship. They should listen to him/her rather than asserting themselves.
- You need to look sexy for your partner. He/she expects that from you.
- You are nothing unless you have a relationship and get married.
- You worry that people will think you can't get a partner.
- You need a partner in your life to complete you.
- There is one perfect person for you out there; you just need to find them.
- You just want a Sugar Daddy/Mama to take care of you.
- You need to be in control of a relationship to feel safe.
- Other women/men are waiting to steal your partner. You can't trust even your good friends because they have no shame when it comes to getting a mate.
- You have been waiting for that knight in shining armor to sweep you off your feet!
- Being alone is the worst situation to be in.
- Love is forever and your partner will be there for you always.
- It's better to be in a relationship where the man loves the woman more, rather than the woman loving the man more.
- You need to make your partner happy and love him/her more than you love yourself.
- When you are in love, you trust the other person 100 percent.
- Your partner should intuitively know what you need in the relationship.

Beliefs we use against ourselves in parenting:

- Once you are a parent, you have to give up everything else in your life.
- A parent is self-sacrificing. Everyone else comes first and then he/she can look toward his/her own needs.

- The only way to really raise your children well is if there are two parents involved.
- Even if you are unhappy in your marriage, you would rather live with your partner than get divorced and have to raise your kids alone.
- You have to stay in your bad relationship because your partner puts food on the table and you could never do it alone. Even if he/she yells at you in front of the kids, at least they have a nice home and no financial problems.
- You would give anything up for your children.
- You don't have time to exercise or take care of yourself because of the kids; it will just have to wait until they are older.
- Your kids don't appreciate all the things you have given up for them over the years, but when they are older they will.
- No one is going to want to date someone with kids, so why bother losing weight or trying to make yourself look good?

Beliefs we use against ourselves sexually:

- Your partner should know what you want sexually; you should not have to say anything.
- If you tell your partner what you want, he/she will think you are weird or that you have had a lot of partners in the past.
- You are afraid to say the things you want your partner to try because your partner will think you are kinky or odd.
- You should not ask your partner to change positions because it's more important that he/she is satisfied. You don't want him/her to think you are selfish.
- A woman should be able have an orgasm from intercourse alone so you'd better not let your husband know that you're not having an orgasm that way; you don't want him to think you are frigid.
- You refuse to touch yourself in front of your partner because it's embarrassing.
- Anything other than sex in the missionary position is wrong.
- If your partner wants to have sex, it's your duty to be available.

- It's easier to just let your partner do his/her thing than to get into it with him/her about his/her lousy technique.
- Masturbation is wrong; if your partner is satisfying you, you shouldn't need to do that.
- Sex is just disgusting and gross.
- Looking at pictures of naked men/women when you are in a relationship is cheating on your partner.

Beliefs we use against ourselves spiritually:

- You need an intermediary between yourself and Spirit.
- Only people who can totally devote their lives to Spirit can be in an enlightened place.
- If you had the right teacher, he/she would be able to fix you.
- A real spiritual teacher is one who renounces all worldly things.
- Spiritual people have no sense of humor and are boring.
- A spiritual person has to meditate many hours each day and you don't have that kind of time.
- A spiritual person devotes their life to others like Mother Theresa.
- A real spiritual person lives in an ashram, not in the world.
- You have to go to Church or Temple in order to connect with Spirit.
- Spiritually enlightened people are not accessible.
- A spiritual person always behaves perfectly.
- God is above you and will punish you for your sins by sending you to hell.
- You can never be loved by Spirit because of what you have done in your life.
- Only true spiritual teachings are given for free; everything else is a fraud.

You may read these lists and agree with many of the things that are written. But the key here is to see with great clarity and honesty that none of these beliefs have any absolute truth to them. Sit with them a while and meditate on their purpose. They are just points of view and most of them come from fear, not love. All of them ultimately create suffering, not joy. These beliefs act like viruses within your program and direct the way you live your life. Remember: We create concepts and their associated beliefs.

I recognize that I am challenging things that you have taken to believe as truth, perhaps for your whole life. Just take a breath and rather than arguing with me in your head, see if you are able to let go of what you believe and expand your point of view about what is possible. In the next chapter, I will work with examples from these lists in order to further explain how this process works.

## *Rewriting False Concepts*

*If you change your point of view* from fear to love, most of what you used to believe will fall apart before your very eyes. Why? Because only truth can grow in a garden of love and only lies can grow in a garden of fear. In this chapter, I will demonstrate how you can challenge what you believe so you can figure out for yourself which beliefs are not supporting you in your life. To do so I randomly picked several beliefs from the previous chapter to illustrate this procedure. I recommend you do this with a great sense of humor and make it an engaging activity. Here we go!

*"Other women/men are waiting to steal my partner. I can't trust even my good friends because they have no shame when it comes to getting a mate."*

Many people would agree with this statement because they have seen it happen to others, have experienced it directly in their own lives, or have been taught this attitude from their parents, friends, or the TV. But let's look at the beliefs that underlie these statements. There is an assumption here that we "own" our partners, whether we're dating or married. (Otherwise, how can you "steal" someone?) Is this statement really the truth? Can we ever own anyone or anything in this life? No, we can't. Death owns everything in this life and everything we have is only on loan. You can lose your home, your job, your clothes, your money, your family, your friends, your partner, and even your own life at any time. So if another man or woman is with your partner, it's not because you "lost" anything or anyone; it's because your partner wants to be with that other person. And how do you know what life and Spirit have in store for you? The other man or woman could have just facilitated the best thing that has ever happened to you! He or she removed a partner from your life who didn't belong there. But if you believe that losing your partner is a "bad" thing and you judge this experience as terrible,

*"Ideas, like individuals, live and die. They flourish, according to their nature, in one soil or climate and droop in another. They are the vegetation of the mental world."*

— MACNEILE
DIXON

then you will not have the eyes to see how Spirit's expressing itself in your life.

The belief that you can actually "lose" a partner comes from the fear of losing someone whom you believe is yours or whom you need to survive. This affects the way you see life, distorts your point of view, and steals your clarity. It's even something that you can use to abuse yourself with. For example, if you believe you own the people in your life, it will be easy for you to blame yourself, to say it was your looks, how you performed in bed, your personality, or whatever else you can think of if they happen to leave you.

The other big lie here is that the other person — the person who leaves a relationship — should be ashamed of himself or herself. This is not about having judgment about others. Everyone is responsible for their half of a relationship, but other people are ultimately going to do what they want to do. Out of kindness and respect for each other, it would be ideal if the partner who wants to leave the relationship could be open about wanting to be elsewhere, but not everyone is capable of such honesty. If you find yourself in this situation, remember that your partner's actions are not about you, they're about your partner and it would behoove you to not take those actions personally.

Lastly this belief talks about trust. If we put our trust in others, we're assuming that they're going to do or say exactly what we believe they're going to do or say. The truth is the only thing we can trust is that people are going to do whatever they are going to do, not necessarily what we think they are going to do! There's a big difference here! This doesn't mean you need to be a suspicious person; it means that it's in your best interest to have no expectations regarding the actions of others. Then you'll never have a reason to be surprised at their actions, nor will you have to feel bad and victimize yourself for trusting them.

After I had been studying this work for a few years, I had a talk with my teacher about this very thing. I was recapitulating my two previous marriages to see my responsibility in both situations. He suggested I go back to my second husband and thank him for having an affair and leaving me. I was shocked at first by his request! But then he said that if my ex-husband had not been directed by Spirit moving through him to embark on a new relationship, I would have never left him to pursue this Toltec path, and never changed myself and my life the way I did. Gosh, I never thought about it from that point of view. (Of course neither had my ex-husband until I thanked him!)

As a result of my second divorce, it took me 5 years to recover enough to have another serious relationship. Had I had this new point of view at that time, I would have said to my ex-husband, "I wish you the best in life. Thank you for the great years we had together, and for the opportunity to love and learn from you." I would have been able to let go with grace and not have abused myself for the following 5 years. Having the point of view of gratitude certainly makes a big difference!

Are you ready to de-program another belief?

*"It's necessary to be thin to succeed. Even if one must use laxatives or vomit to prevent gaining weight, it's worth it."*

As you might be able to guess here, the key belief behind this statement is that we need to look differently than the way we are. So how are you supposed to change the frame you were born with? Spirit resides in the physical body, and it's a kindness to treat it with respect and care. You have one body for the rest of your life, whatever type it happens to be, whether you currently like it or not. So basically you have two choices: Either love that body or hate it and abuse it.

Truthfully, no matter what others may think of you and your looks, it only really matters what you believe about yourself. If you have absolute self-love and respect for yourself, you will be happy about being you. If you are using society's beliefs about what you should look like in order to abuse your physical body, perhaps it's time to examine those beliefs. You'll find that they are based in fear — fear of not being accepted by society, fear of not finding a partner in life, or fear of not securing a good job or the proper friends. The belief that your body is not "good enough" will act as a virus, affecting the way you see your relationships, the situations you choose to put yourself in, and your general level of happiness. There has been enough press about eating disorders for us understand the life-threatening effects that repetitive dieting, anorexia and bulimia can have on our bodies. And this applies not just to women who traditionally have suffered from eating and body image disorders, but also to men. All of us need to forget the "perfect body" hype and learn to love ourselves — and each other — just the way we are.

Ok, here's another one:

*"I need a partner in my life to complete me. I feel depressed when my other friends have a partner and I don't. There must be something wrong with me."*

Let's look at the beliefs behind these statements. First of all, every person is a whole person; there are no halves walking around, so no person can ever complete you. It's our lack of love for ourselves that has us searching for love in all the wrong places — outside of ourselves! When we suffer from lack of self-love, we give the responsibility for our happiness away to others and look to them to fulfill our needs. If another person gives us love, we're happy and we'll do anything for that love, even compromise ourselves and go against our integrity. How many times have you been in a relationship that you knew wasn't a good idea? And why did you still pursue it? Was it desperation, wanting someone so badly that you would settle for someone who you knew might go against you, and hurt or abuse you?

If you feel depressed when you're not dating someone, ask yourself what is causing you to feel this way. You are using this belief — that you need someone else in your life — to make yourself sad. If you have this belief, then you may also have some other related issues, too. For example, if you are depressed without a partner then it's likely that you don't enjoy going out and doing things by yourself. If you're always staying home by yourself when you don't have a partner, who is stopping you from enjoying all that life has to offer, you or the missing partner? It's up to you to make the choice to not believe these things anymore, to rewrite your beliefs to be more supportive of yourself.

It's possible to be absolutely happy never having a partner your entire life as long as you have no need to find your happiness outside of yourself. Society has many beliefs regarding having a partner and there's a lot of pressure to conform to those rules. Believe me, there is no white knight, only a good fairy tale about him! Be your own best friend and white knight to yourself. Start by honestly looking at what you believe about relationships and eliminating the thoughts that come from a place of fear.

**"My kids don't appreciate all the things I have given up for them over the years but when they're older, they will."**

Martyrdom is only romantic on television, not in real life. There are many self-defeating beliefs in this statement. First is a belief that you have to "give up" things for your children. Yes, children are very time-consuming. They require a lot of attention, and more importantly, love. So maybe you will not finish that college degree you desire in 4 years. Maybe it will take 6 or 8 years instead, but you can still do it. Having kids is about balance, not about sacrifice. We're always setting priorities in our lives. When you have children, they become more important and something else becomes less important, but you don't have to give up anything except your expectations that things are going to look like they did before your children came around.

Kids are amazingly astute and observant. If your kids see that you have lived your life as a doormat, I can assure you they will not appreciate that when they get older. On the other hand, if a child sees that you have self-love and can accomplish your dreams and goals under challenging circumstances, they will learn the same for themselves. What a gift that is!

There is a belief that a parent should put his or her family before themselves. This used to be considered to be the way a good parent behaved. But truly a parent who loves themselves so much that they have created balance in their life is sending a more wholesome message to their children. Kids are less likely to walk all over parents who have clearly defined their boundaries and are more likely to learn gratitude, appreciation, and fortitude. It's important to have time with your children, but it's as important to love them and demonstrate to them how to love themselves. This is something you can't explain to them; you need to live it in your own life by loving yourself. Take some time to re-write these beliefs to support a more healthy and loving lifestyle.

***"I am afraid to say what things I want my partner to try sexually because my partner will think I am kinky or odd."***

It's amazing how many people are afraid to embrace their sexuality completely and own up to the power associated with it. Humans are animals, just like all the others on this earth, programmed to reproduce the species. We all have the urge to have sex because this desire is built into our genes to protect our species survival. So why do we create such a big deal around this natural phenomenon? We have so many hang-ups and rules that interfere with our enjoyment of one of the inherent qualities of being present in a physical body.

Our old puritanical beliefs have carried forward many generations and are still affecting our ability to enjoy our bodies. There is nothing wrong with asking your partner to do something that brings you pleasure. You both have a right to enjoy yourselves, and both of you can ask each other for what feels good. Not every human is exactly alike, nor can anyone assume what another human being enjoys or desires, so if you don't ask, you certainly will not receive. If your partner has no desire to pleasure you the way you wish and you've discussed your needs kindly and clearly, then perhaps it's time to get a new partner.

When we couple physically, it's an opportunity for us to show our partner in yet another way how happy we are to have them in our lives. It's our pleasure to see them feel good, and vice-versa! The only reason you could think that asking your partner for what you want is not appropriate is because you believe what you want is not normal. I doubt you could ask for anything that another human hasn't already thought of! Of course, I am making an assumption that you are not asking for something that goes against yourself or is physically harmful or dangerous to you or your partner. If that's the case, then you need to investigate why you want to be abused instead of loved.

Also, watch yourself carefully to make sure you don't use sex as a means to manipulate your partner and have control in your relationship. If you know that you do this, do your best to stop it immediately. Change and rewrite whatever beliefs this behavior is coming from and keep your issues and corrupt files out of the bedroom. Nothing will ruin a relationship faster than sexual manipulation.

Being in a physical body is an incredible experience and blessing. We receive so much pleasure from our five senses if we allow ourselves to enjoy and be present in our bodies. Just feeling the wind on the hairs of our skin, eating a ripe juicy dripping peach, gazing at a perfect sunset, or listening to a bird singing is enough to be in bliss! When you make love with your partner, it's an opportunity to not only make love on the level of the human animal, but also to merge and make love on the level of the divine. But to do this you must be able to love yourself and others unconditionally and not be afraid to express yourself physically.

*"Spiritual people engage in certain practices that I don't believe in and/or I don't have time for. A spiritual person has to meditate many hours daily and I don't have that kind of time."*

For as many people as you could interview, you would find different opinions and beliefs about what Spirit and spirituality is to them. Some of those beliefs would be coming from love and others from fear. Many of us have been taught to see Spirit as a man with a beard sitting in a big chair above and separate from us ready to condemn us to hell for our transgressions. This image is manipulative in nature, threatening us with fear of condemnation. To transcend these kinds of beliefs it's necessary for us to have a direct experience with Spirit ourselves. This way we come to experience Spirit inside us and outside of us and know in the most personal of ways that we're part of the larger consciousness, like a drop of water originating from an ocean without boundaries, completely infinite.

We're all spiritual people whether we believe it or not, as Spirit's in all beings. Just because you work a job, get paid, and come home to a partner and children, does that make you less spiritual than Mother Theresa? Is the job of raising children not a spiritual endeavor? How do we judge what is more or less spiritual? If you are expressing the love and joy within you and sharing yourself, that is spiritual. If you are working in your dream job and uplifting those around you with your happiness, that is spiritual. If you are living your life authentically from your integrity, that is spiritual. In my eyes, if you are living, you are a spiritual person and every aspect of your life has its purpose.

Yes, it's lovely to meditate in silence in an ashram, but you can meditate while ironing, walking and driving your car. It doesn't have to look a certain way. You don't need to go to a temple to pray to that which is within you at all times. A beautiful field of flowers can be as inspiring as a church or temple service. You don't need a Priest or a Rabbi to connect you to the Spirit that lives inside you, although the community of a church or temple can be lovely and extremely supportive. You don't have to give your power away to any teacher, guide, guru, or preacher because you are no different than they are.

No one has a special audience with Spirit as if it was an individual person you could make an appointment with! You don't have to give away your favorite things to be spiritual, but it's important to understand their impermanence, ultimate unimportance, and detach from your need to constantly acquire more and more things. Death can take away your possessions at any time but that will not make you less wealthy, as true wealth is measured by the amount of love you possess in your heart — not by the number of possessions you own or the amount of money you have.

Spiritual people are not "perfect," whatever that means according to society. They have some days when they practice love, compassion, and kindness more effectively than on other days. It's the overall practice of spirituality in one's life that is most important and not the judgment of one's performance. After all, if you practice unconditional love on a regular basis but you are a bit cranky one day, should you judge yourself to be not spiritual for having had a bad day? If you use the human concept of "God" to judge and punish yourself for the things you hate about yourself or for the things you regret doing, it's your programming that is punishing you, not "God." For me, fear does not equal Spirit. How can the practice of unconditional love and joy come from a "God" that instills fear? To me there is no logic in that and it's plainly contradictory and is reflective of the way humans have interpreted the sacred books of our great spiritual teachers. (In other words I am not illustrating the actions of God here, only how we use what we believe about God to hurt ourselves.)

Lastly, I often hear that if you have to pay for spiritual teachings, they are not truth. Our churches, temples, and spiritual teachers must receive income and/or donations to pay their staff and bills, just like everyone else. Teaching is an energetic activity. If you give of your time and energy, it's reasonable to have an exchange of energy in return. If you have this belief, consider how many opportunities for self-growth you've missed because of this.

There is much truth out there that Spirit shares with us constantly, but we don't have the eyes to see this because our beliefs and mind spam prevents us from taking action based on those truths. Our fear-based beliefs form a veil of illusion that separates us from our true source. I encourage you to question everything you believe on this subject and whether it's truly serving your higher self. Look deeply within your heart for what is truth for you and not to what lies within your programming. Let go of everything you were taught regarding Spirit and let your inner wisdom, integrity, and intuition guide you. The key is to have an experience of divine consciousness for yourself; that way, you're not just listening to some teacher standing on a soapbox preaching about what they believe. This is wisdom of the heart, your own experience of enlightenment and true knowing. I would encourage you to feel this for yourself and not just believe what I or anyone else tells you on the topic just because they've published a book or because they stand on a pulpit!

Tearing apart our beliefs and finding the viruses that hide within them is a fascinating process. This is the first step, learning to question everything and to take inventory. Now that we have a little background into the inventory, we will go a little deeper into this process in the next section.

## *Action list to help us challenge what we believe:*

- Either by yourself or with a group of friends, take each belief listed in the last chapter, and tear them apart as I demonstrated for you in the examples above. Have fun and use your imagination!

- Ask yourself where these beliefs came from and/or who gave them to you in the first place.

- Also spend some time looking at the examples of core beliefs in this chapter and see how they relate to you in your life and what other beliefs you may have that are related to them.

- For each belief, ask the question, "Is this belief based in fear or is it based in love?"

- Notice how from a particular point of view the beliefs may seem valid — but realize they aren't going to create joy and happiness in your life, no matter how much you justify them.

Please feel free to add whatever beliefs you can think of that were not listed in each category. This exercise should prove to be quite enlightening and challenging!

# Section 3

## *Quarantining The Viruses And Isolating Damaged Files*

*"I believe all suffering is caused by ignorance. People inflict pain on others in the selfish pursuit of their happiness or satisfaction. Yet true happiness comes from a sense of peace and contentment, which in turn must be achieved through the cultivation of altruism, of love and compassion, and elimination of ignorance, selfishness and greed."*

*— THE DALAI LAMA*

***Section 2 focused on getting to*** the bottom of what we believe. In Section 3, we'll learn how to halt the program in its tracks and begin to counteract the damage it causes in our daily lives. This is not something that can be done passively; it involves concentration and action!

This section is very hands-on. You'll find a worksheet to help you break down which emotions you are feeling and why, as well as some examples from common experiences which will help you understand how to identify and embrace what you are feeling so that you can process though your emotions and the beliefs that are causing them.

# Chapter 10

## *Tools For Cleaning Up Your Program*

***If you want to remove a corrupted file*** from your home computer, in most cases, you can just delete it. In the human mind, however, memory prevents us from getting rid of damaged files so easily. In fact, you can't ever truly delete a file from your mind, short of taking a knife and sticking it in your brain. (Of course, this is not an effective way to approach the issue unless you consider brain death an option, but I don't!) Instead, we must quarantine the files corrupted with viruses and write new ones. The old files — filled with fear-based beliefs, anger, and resentments — will always be present, so you might ask, "What is going to stop them from asserting themselves again in the future?" If you stop investing your attention and personal power in them, they will lose their ability to control you. Those files will always have the ability to "pop-up" on the computer screen in your mind, but just keep pressing the "delete" button when they come up and set your mind spam controls on high, and eventually, they will stop returning. The processes of letting go by using forgiveness and detaching from your expectations and beliefs will ensure your success.

*"Not everything that is faced can be changed, but nothing can be changed until it's faced."*

*— JAMES BALDWIN*

Replacing the corrupted files with new files is an involved process and includes taking responsibility, losing our expectations, not taking others' comments and behaviors to heart, and learning to forgive. I consider each step a "tool" for cleaning up the mind's program and have separated these four topics into subsections here in order to give each the attention it deserves.

### TOOL #1: Learning to take responsibility.

There's a lot of talk these days about taking responsibility for one's actions, yet we see that people are constantly blaming everything on everyone else. Statements like "You're driving me crazy," "You're giving me a headache," and "You make me sick" are pervasive in our society and put the onus of responsibility on the other person. Can anybody give us any of these physical ailments? No! We can only create these emotions within ourselves of our own accord. If we use this type of language, we're using our word to give our power away to another person. In addition, we make ourselves the victim every time we speak like this. We may understand that we're responsible for the co-creation of our life, but it means nothing until we take action and responsibility for our thoughts, actions, and choices.

> *"Action springs not from thought, but from a readiness for responsibility."*
> — DEITRICH BONHOEFFER

In our society, we're actually rewarded when we blame things on others and renege on our responsibilities. If we slip and fall on ice, it's someone else's fault.  If we get sick at a restaurant, the place owes us a dinner. If we don't get better in "X" number of days, we want to blame our doctor. People sue the cigarette companies for lung disease when we have known for years that it's not healthy to smoke. And how many advertisements are there for lawyers asking us to sue for every conceivable situation? It's all always the fault of another. Yes, we all wish for flat, non-slippery streets, food without bacteria, speedy recoveries from our illnesses, non-carcinogenic cigarettes, and an otherwise perfectly safe world, but this isn't how life works. Let's say that I slip on some ice outside of a store. I have to acknowledge and take responsibility for the fact that I may have been wearing shoes that contributed to my slipping, or perhaps my attention was focused elsewhere. I can't blame these things on someone else. Therefore, the store owner does not owe me anything.

We can also see these concepts illustrated in our interpersonal relationships. We love to concern ourselves with what we believe is wrong with the other person. I remember talking to a woman who had recently ended a relationship with her boyfriend. She said her ex was childish, inconsiderate, and self-centered, and that he needed to work on himself; in fact, she had advised him to see a therapist. When I tried to get her to focus on her side of the relationship, she kept migrating over to his side of things. Finally I said, "It doesn't matter what he did or what his issues are. You entered into the relationship knowing what he was like, didn't you? And even if you couldn't see that clearly when the relationship started, no one was stopping you from leaving as soon as you had clarity. This is your opportunity to take responsibility for your own issues and drama instead of pointing your finger at him."

And what about all of the other situations that cause us to become angry with someone else? If someone is driving slowly in front of you and you start beeping or yelling at them because you're late, isn't it your fault for not leaving the house earlier? If your life is crazy, isn't it because you chose to have a hundred things going on at once? If your staff keeps quitting, isn't it time to stop blaming it on bad employees and start looking at what you are doing to help create this problem? The world is constantly mirroring information back to us regarding our actions. This is why Toltecs believe in taking responsibility for what is theirs and resolving life's issues without getting upset, rather than blaming their circumstances on others. To do this, we must put our denial system aside and give our self-importance and ego a much-needed rest. If we open our eyes and take responsibility for what we're doing, we will see astounding things about ourselves.

> *It's important to recognize how we're co-creating our entire reality in every moment. We're absolutely responsible for everything that is going on in our lives and all the activities we've chosen to participate in: our schedules, where we live, what jobs we have chosen, who we're in relationship with, our financial commitments, our friends, who we portray ourselves as in the world, how we behave, the situations we get ourselves into and how we treat ourselves. The key is to recognize that your program is making these life choices for you, and your program, unfortunately, is filled with virus-ridden beliefs and lies. The decisions you make in every moment of your life reflect the level of corruption of your program.*

Our universe works on the scientific principle of action-reaction: For every action there is an equal and opposite reaction. So why do we keep taking the same actions and expecting that different reactions will occur? We can never ask any other person to change, nor are we responsible for changing anyone else. (We can hardly manage to change ourselves — what makes us think we can change another person?) When you take action, look at the results honestly. Are they what you are looking for? Are your actions creating love and joy in your life or anger, suffering, and drama? If you keep creating drama, frustration, and arguments, then take responsibility and change your actions!

### *Action list to support the practice of taking responsibility:*

#### *Catch yourself in the act:*
As soon as you see yourself about to blame something on another person or situation, stop immediately! It doesn't matter whether you are about to blame your tardiness on the traffic or weather, your headache on another person, your bad day on your boss, or your failing marriage on your husband. Look at your side of the story and how you may have helped cause the situation.

*Choose a reaction:*

You decide how to react to every situation in your life. Take responsibility for your moods and recognize that if you are not happy, you are the only person who can change that. When you see your mood shifting, stop and ask yourself why are you giving your happiness away at that moment?

*Determine where your energy is going:*

Your energy flows where your attention goes. How much time every day do you devote to solving other people's problems and issues? If it's more than 5 minutes, you are wasting energy that would be better spent on yourself. It's not your responsibility to fix anyone else's problems. This is your program's way of getting out of dealing with its own issues by diverting your focus.

*Watch your verbiage and behavior:*

If people don't react to you the way you feel they should, take responsibility for what is coming out of your mouth and the way you're acting. Pay attention to what you're really saying and doing, since your actions are the cause of the unpleasant reactions you're getting.

TOOL #2: **Letting go of expectations.**

Every time something does not go our way, we get upset, frustrated, worried, or we find ourselves in a place of drama and emotional reaction. If the traffic causes us to be late for work, we're annoyed. If our children don't do what we want, we're angry. If we don't get a free meal in the restaurant we supposedly got sick in, we get uppity and refuse to eat there again. If our partner is unfaithful, it causes us to go into a jealous rage.

What is the common thread in each of these examples? Expectations! The truth is that things are always happening in life that go against what we believe is right or the way we think things should be. So if we know this, and have all experienced this thousands of times in our life, then why do we still get upset when things don't go our way? Why do we insist on needing to control every little aspect of our lives?

Once the program of the mind is structured, everything we experience is filtered through and measured against what is already present in the program. This is what creates our ever-present expectations. Just because we believe that things in life are supposed to look a certain way doesn't mean that life is going to comply. We now know that the content of the mind is quite arbitrary, so it's not reasonable to expect that the universe would be subject to our personal program's rules. It's all right if we can't control every outcome to every situation in our lives. Our world will not fall apart and we don't have to be scared. We can trust that if we have done our best with our actions, the universe will give us a reaction that is most appropriate, even if we don't see it that way.

Certainly it's easy to see how the monumental events in life, like a divorce or getting fired, could cause us to give our happiness away. We expect marriages and jobs to last forever (or at least as long as we want them to), so when they end unexpectedly, it can be quite a shock to the system. But it's even more significant and devastating when we get upset, day-in and day-out, over the little things that don't go according to plan! This way of reacting to everything in life is just a habitual way of behaving and a waste and total drain of personal power and energy. Do your best to catch yourself and your expectations before you react strongly and negatively to anything. At first, this will be very hard to do, but eventually, you'll be able to see the self-created drama coming and stop yourself from reacting. It just takes practice.

Magic comes from detaching from your expectations about everything and letting life happen on life's terms. You may think what I'm saying is a bit strange, but try this for yourself – you'll see your life shift before your eyes and become effortless. No matter what happens, you'll just take action, finish what needs to be done, and move on — without the drama and victimization of failed expectations. Your happiness quotient will increase significantly and people will perceive something different in you. (Remember the law of action-reaction?) Your joy will cause people to want to do things for you and to want to be around you. This is the magic I am talking about!

### *Action list to support the practice of detaching from your expectations:*

#### *Take a time out:*
When you feel yourself getting upset because things are not going the way you believe they should be, remove yourself from the situation. Take a deep breath, clear your mind, and ask yourself what your expectations are in this situation and if you are willing to detach from them in order to be happy. Would you rather be right (according to your program) or happy?

#### *Turn things around:*
When things are not going the way your program would like them to go, take a chance and handle the situation in a different way than you normally would. Take an action that's opposite from your normal behavior and see what the results are. You might be pleasantly surprised.

(These opposite behaviors are called not-doings, and are discussed in greater detail in Chapter 7.)

**TOOL #3:   Not taking things to heart.**

The third tool necessary for cleaning out the mind's program is to learn not to take the things that others do or say to heart. This will help you release your expectations of others and give you emotional immunity to others' actions. If you get in the habit of doing this, you will cut down on the amount of "letting go" you have to do. After all, if you stop getting angry at others for their actions, you won't have to keep letting go of your anger, frustrations, and resentments. Once you go through the process of forgiving everything and everyone from your past, not taking anything to heart will help you to not have anything or anyone to forgive in the future.

> *"To be wronged is nothing unless you continue to remember it."*
> — *CONFUCIUS*

Let's say, for example, that you get fired from your job, and your mom reacts to this news by saying, "See? I told you that job would never work out. You never stay employed – you're always getting fired!" You immediately go into reaction to her opinion of you, engaging the same old emotional reactions and behaviors resulting in your arguing with her until both of you are exhausted. You wonder if she'll ever accept and love you just the way you are. You're so hurt by her comments that you never take the time to honestly ask yourself if what she is saying has any truth to it, nor do you ask yourself if you are guilty of having the same judgmental attitude toward your mother by not accepting and loving her just the way she is. You're totally focused on the perceived injustice of her comments towards you and indulging in your victim's point of view.

As we know, what exists in our own mind is not the same as what exists in anyone else's mind. As a result, we can only express what our program believes. Your mom can only see you through the eyes of her own experience and programming. Are your mom's comments about you the truth? Well, they aren't any more or less the truth than your comments and opinions about her! What we believe seems like the absolute truth to us, but it's only truth from our personal point of view.

If we know this, we can have more patience and understanding for the things that the people around us are saying and doing. We can see that they're expressing themselves from the world that exists in their own mind. We can listen to their words and appreciate their point of view, but we don't have to subscribe to their opinions. In that way, we share our communications instead of arguing about them. When we're dogmatic about our point of view, the only result can be conflict (which, on the world scale, is the reason we're always at war). This conflict comes from not having respect for other people's beliefs and opinions, and from believing only we're right, both of which are an expression of our self-importance and egocentric nature.

> *We can always clarify what others are saying to us by asking questions rather than getting upset about what others are saying or doing. That's what clear communication is about.*

The reason for taking your mother personally in the above example is because you want her to see you the way you want to be seen. On a much deeper level, you believe what she's saying, and that's what really hurts. But on the surface, your denial system will not allow you to admit this to yourself and instead will make you focus solely on the injustice of her comments. She's touching your core beliefs that you're never going to amount to anything, that you're inadequate, not capable of success in life, and not lovable.

For you not to take anything to heart, you must have absolute faith and love for yourself. Then it won't matter what anyone says to you, whether it's an insult or a compliment! Both are simply expressions of how another person is seeing you. (And just because it's a compliment doesn't mean it's any more true than an insult!) If someone says something hurtful, you don't have to take it to heart, EVER! Even if someone physically hurts you, it's not about you; it's because their belief system told them it was the right thing to do, even though it caused you harm. Believe me, unfortunate things happen in life and everything is not always about you. It's very self-centered for us to think in this way.

Adopting the attitude of not taking anything to heart is not meant to empower you to put your issues onto others by saying "Hey, that's your problem and I don't have to listen to you." No, when someone expresses their point of view, it behooves you to listen to see if there is a message that's important for you to hear. They could be reflecting something to you that you don't have awareness of because your denial system won't allow you to acknowledge it on your own. For instance, if someone says, "You're very disturbing at work because you talk so loudly," you don't have to get hurt by that comment. Instead, objectively acknowledge what the other person has to say and see if there is any possible truth in their comment.

Someone recently asked me why we get upset even when we know that someone is saying something to us that is not true. This happens because on a deeper level, we believe them and we get defensive to protect ourselves, like in the example I used above with the mom. Imagine if my girlfriend said to me, "Sheri, you look too thin in that suit. It doesn't give you any shape." If I get upset at her, it's because I believe I do look too thin (I'm the walking talking stick-ball bat – remember?) and I don't want to be hearing it from her. The adult part of my program may logically know that statement is not necessarily the truth, but if the childhood part of my program still has a contaminated self-worth file filled with beliefs that I am ugly,

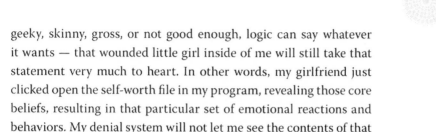

geeky, skinny, gross, or not good enough, logic can say whatever it wants — that wounded little girl inside of me will still take that statement very much to heart. In other words, my girlfriend just clicked open the self-worth file in my program, revealing those core beliefs, resulting in that particular set of emotional reactions and behaviors. My denial system will not let me see the contents of that self-worth file easily because it will engage immediately and as a result I will say something like, "She obviously is jealous of what I have on today, Cindy can be such a witch." I take her comments to heart and blame her rather than taking responsibility for my emotional wounding and corrupt beliefs.

> *Every time you go into reaction about something, you're actually giving that person your personal power and happiness. By reacting we're giving them the ability to make us angry or unhappy, frustrated or jealous. If we're aware of this then why would we want to give another person charge of our emotional state of being? If we give our power away to another person they will use it for their benefit. And of course this would be against us in most cases. This doesn't mean people are purposely or inherently evil. No, it's just that people do what suits them first because they don't have awareness. This is why we must forgive others because they know not what they do.*

Another way we take the actions of others to heart is when we're ending a relationship. We want to control when our loved ones enter and exit our lives, but love doesn't work that way. Whether your significant other had an affair or simply decided to leave you, it was their decision; it's not about you. We have been socialized to get very emotional, to seek revenge, and to blame it all on our partner. (Just watch any soap opera or TV drama; they show us exactly how to do it!) On top of it all, we want to confront this person and find out why they are doing this to us, as though anyone can do anything to us! Of course, we're inadvertently affected by our beloved's departure, but he or she is just acting in their best own interest according to what their program is telling them. It doesn't matter if we think their actions are right or wrong, and judging them or taking those actions personally won't change anything.

Many people have asked me why I don't think it's important to find out why their partner is leaving. This is because you never know if the other person is going to tell you the whole truth, whatever that may be. I think you're better off evaluating the relationship honestly by yourself or with a therapist or mentor. Ask yourself; "What was my part in this relationship? What did I do that I could change for the future? Did I have expectations that were unreasonable? Were there signs about this relationship that I was unwilling to see because I was so infatuated? Was I always defending my point of view? Was I always in reaction because of things that happened in my past? Was my communication with my partner clear? Was I always imposing my belief system on my partner?"

You can only answer these questions for yourself, and you can only take responsibility for your half of the relationship. In asking your ex these questions, you could get answers that are detrimental to your personal growth, or you may receive a response fabricated to take any responsibility off of themselves. Sometimes, getting that type information can be quite dangerous, especially if you are at that point in your life where you haven't isolated all of your self-sabotaging beliefs and agreements. You could believe everything that person shares with you, take that information to heart, and blame yourself for things that were not your responsibility.

### *Action list to support the practice of not taking things to heart:*

#### *Choose a person a day:*
Pick one person today, and no matter what they say or do, detach from the need to argue with them. Resist defending your point of

view and blaming everything on them. Reflect on the reasons why you become upset with this person, and see if you can list the beliefs that are responsible for your emotional reactions. Are they truth?

### To abuse, or not to abuse?:

Every time you are about to take someone's actions to heart ask yourself the following questions: Do I want to abuse my physical body with my emotional reactions because of someone else's words or actions? How much do I really love myself? Are the other person's words or actions worth making myself sick and losing my personal power over? Am I addicted to creating drama in my life in this way?

### Find the message:

Once you get the hang of not going into reaction to what people say and do, the next step is to ask yourself if what they are saying contains a message for you. Do your very best to be objective and to tell yourself the truth rather than going into denial. They may be seeing something in you that you're not aware of that can be of great benefit to your process and growth.

**TOOL #4: The value of forgiveness.**

Forgiveness is a beautiful human concept, but how many of us are able to truly forgive? We can never achieve personal freedom without first mastering this skill. I've met many people who have been working on themselves for years and have identified the viruses in their program that have created the unhealthy patterns in their lives, yet they're stuck, doing workshop after workshop, never having completed the process of detaching from their fears, their anger, and their pain. They haven't replaced their damaged files containing their self-sabotaging routines with new files filled with healthy beliefs, nor have they forgiven themselves or the people who have hurt them. They still carry their resentments like yokes around their necks.

> *At one of my retreats, a person said to me, "At every workshop I go to they tell me I have to let go of my fear-based beliefs, fears, anger, and resentments that I'm holding onto and forgive both myself and others in my life. What does that really mean? I keep doing these forgiveness exercises and trying to let go, but I just don't know what that means or how to do it!" Letting go is like trying to shake a piece of flypaper off of your hand. You flick your hand over and over again, saying, "Get off!" to the paper, yet the paper is still stuck. It takes using your other hand to detach the paper from your skin to remove it for good. Only by the action of detachment can you truly let go. Stop holding on to your fear-based beliefs, fears, anger, and resentments and stop flicking! Decide that you don't want to hold on to that stuff anymore and "let go!"*

So what is the secret to forgiving and letting go? The key is to forgive from the heart, not from the mind. If you have an emotional reaction in the presence of a particular person, that is your heart's way of telling you that you haven't resolved your issues with them. Take some time to journal the story of what you experienced with that person. Read what you've written, and be objective: If someone else read your story, would they say that you sound victimized, resentful, vengeful, and angry? If so, you haven't forgiven the other person; you still believe your story, your point of view, and your lies.

The important thing is to have awareness of what has transpired between yourself and the other person and to be able to tell yourself the truth about it. That doesn't mean you have to agree with their point of view, what they did, or how they did it; your values and beliefs may be very different from theirs, after all. It just means you will be able to see the whole truth of what happened, and the whole truth encompasses all points of view, not just your own. This applies to even the worst kinds of human interactions: physical, emotional, sexual, and mental abuse, violence, and infidelity. The result of this awareness is being able to have gratitude for everything that has happened in life to bring you to this moment. I know this is a difficult thing to comprehend, especially when most of us feel so self-righteous about the justifications that help to maintain our anger and hate towards those who have abused us.

> *I am suggesting a different way of perceiving life, one without judgment and with the ability to have respect for others' points of view and beliefs, one where you take responsibility for your mind, what it thinks, and as a result, how you choose to react to any situation. When you can truly see the other person's point of view, then you can forgive from the heart. True compassion comes from love that is unconditional and is the place from which forgiveness begins.*

In this process, it's important to forgive not just the other people in our lives but ourselves also, which can be very challenging. Forgive yourself for:

- Using other people in your life to hurt yourself.
- Not having clarity, blaming others, and not taking responsibility for your actions.
- Wounding others and the anger, jealousy, and hate you have directed toward others.
- Participating in situations that went against your integrity.
- Not respecting yourself.
- Not trusting yourself and not having faith in your abilities.
- Trying to control the people you love and telling others what to do.
- Not loving yourself 100 percent just the way you are.

We forgive not because the other person necessarily deserves it, but because we don't want to carry that load around until we die.

Anger, hate, and jealousy will make you old, resentful, and ugly, inside and out. If you can't forgive yourself or others in your life, keep practicing and keep looking at the damaged and corrupted files that you insist on hanging onto. How much do you love and respect yourself? Is it enough to accept the gift of forgiveness?

### *Action list to support the practice of forgiveness:*

#### *Practice forgiveness in the moment:*
As soon as you see yourself having an emotional reaction to someone or something, stop and forgive yourself and the other person for whatever it is they are doing or saying. This is an awareness exercise to help you begin to recognize that the fear-based emotions you are creating within yourself are due to what you believe about the situation, and not from the situation itself. Also, get in the habit of letting go of your anger and resentments immediately, before they start piling up.

#### *Realize that ignorance is not bliss:*
We react, say, and do things to others that they take to heart as often as others do the same to us. Most of the time, we don't realize what we're doing, especially when we think we're doing or saying something for the other person's benefit. In other words, our program feels fully empowered to tell another program what to say or do. Whenever you catch yourself doing this, have compassion for yourself and the other person; forgive and apologize to yourself for your ignorance!

Now let us continue on and see how we can use these tools in our process!

## *Putting Your Tools Into Action*

**As we've discussed** in the previous chapters, our beliefs are not always self-evident and we need to use all the self-awareness tools we can get our hands on to see what's spam and what's truth. In this chapter we have the chance to see how the Four Tools from Chapter 10 (Taking Responsibility, Letting Go Of Expectations, Not Taking Things To Heart, and The Value Of Forgiveness) can be engaged in quarantining those feisty virus-ridden files simply by observing our normal (but not necessarily pleasant) behavior patterns.

In general, human behavior is pretty predictable because we process information and have been domesticated in a similar manner. This is actually an important observation because if you come to truly understand yourself, you will find you're able to understand others much easier. If you observe people carefully, you'll find that they often behave and react in ways that seem out of proportion to the current situation at hand. For example, we see ourselves going into reaction and we want to stop ourselves but we cannot because we do not know the true reasons why we are in reaction. We never look at the beliefs driving these behaviors and the emotional "templates" (the tendency to always demonstrate a particular set of emotions in a particular type of situation) associated with them.

In my own personal life, I always engaged in the same set of emotions when a situation occurred which resembled the relationship between my parents and myself. We can look for those emotional templates as they have recurred over and over again during the epoch movie of our life and see how we keep recreating the same behavioral and emotional patterns without our awareness. This empowers us to change our actions once we realize what we are really reacting to.

*"There is great beauty in going through life without anxiety or fear. Half our fears are baseless, and the other half discreditable."*

— BOVEE

> *My suggestion is for you to milk every life situation you are in absolutely dry of all it has to offer. I used to make a game of identifying my emotional templates. It helped me lighten up and prevented me from getting angry with my unpleasant behaviors. That made it easier to forgive myself and to let any self-judgment go. Every time I would have a reaction, I would say, "Okay, here comes another opportunity for personal growth. Thank you Spirit for having my mother call me today so that I could get pissed off and see what else I need to deal with within myself." As I said before, having a sense of humor is very important on this path.*

I'd like to share with you some actual examples of how we exhibit repetitive patterns of behavior without the awareness of where they actually came from or why we are even behaving in that way. In addition we will see how we engage the same emotional reactions every time certain kinds of life situations appear. To do this we will be looking at the stories of two people, Ralph and Beth. By following their situations you'll have a deeper understanding of what I'm illustrating.

Let's start with Ralph's situation first. Ralph noticed a pattern in his life of getting assigned to every committee, project, or event that came his way. It seemed that he was always the person others depended on to organize something or to get a job done. He enjoyed completing tasks, doing them well, and receiving kudos from all his friends and colleagues, yet he never had free time and always seemed to be busy with other peoples' stuff. It was difficult for him to say no because he felt that no one could do any job as well as he could. (Of course, everyone knew he was the best!) Yet on the other hand he often felt resentful for the amount of work always piled on his plate.

Ralph came to realize that when he was young, he was able to get his parents' attention and love by doing "good things" for his father.

He had five siblings and sometimes felt invisible as a child, but if he helped his father with the chores around the house and got better grades in school than his siblings, he was able to get the attention and approval of his family and even experienced the great feeling of having his siblings be jealous of him. Later in life, he just continued this pattern and was "rewarded" with a good job and his colleagues' respect. Because he was capable of getting things done, everyone continually handed him projects. (You know that saying, "Give a busy person the job and they will always get it done"? That summed up Ralph's abilities.)

Once Ralph realized that, as an adult, he didn't need anyone's attention nor did he need to link his self-worth and self-love to the approval of others, he was able to let those core beliefs go. The realization that his core belief of being invisible had been the driving force behind his hyperactivity his entire life was shocking. In looking at the movie of his life, he was able to see the amount of personal power he invested in proving his virus-ridden beliefs to be true. He also could see that his belief of being the only and best person for the job was a lie or spam, coming from his wanting to be the favorite child when he was young. When he was finally able to see his behavior as a child with clarity and truth, he could then admit to himself that other people were also capable of getting the job done if he gave them the chance. Maybe they would not execute the job exactly like he would, but it still would be completed.

Ralph re-wrote his beliefs to say, "I am perfect and complete the way I am. I no longer need the attention and approval of others to provide evidence to myself that I am lovable and visible." Now whenever a situation presents itself where he is asked to take on new project or job, he asks himself if he has the time and energy to do it and if it will create more fun in his life. If it will only create fatigue and stress, the answer is no! He's not letting his old programming dictate his life anymore. He can take action and make choices rather than being a prisoner of his patterned emotional reactions and behaviors. Ralph took his faith and personal power out of his fear-based beliefs and put them into new beliefs based in self-love and respect. He was able to forgive himself for using other people to hurt himself and to take responsibility for what his old beliefs were creating in his life. Eliminating the need for unhealthy expectations for himself and letting go of his expectations about the way people should do things was a great blessing.

Now let's take a look at Beth's story. Beth had a situation at work where her boss empowered her to get signed contracts from clients by a particular date. When the cutoff date arrived, there was still one client who had not paid attention to deadline due to his personal relationship with her boss. This man felt privileged and figured he could submit the contract when it was convenient for him without suffering the consequences. Beth was really upset because she felt the cutoff date had no meaning if it was not observed by everyone, and she did not want there to be an appearance of favoritism amongst clients. Then she learned that another supposed "friend" of her boss' was going behind her back to avoid signing the contract by speaking directly to her boss after the cutoff date. Beth was furious, but she could not understand why she got so pushed by something that was upsetting but not the end of the world. When she got home, she spent some time journaling how she felt about what had happened that day.

Her journal helped Beth to see a pattern in her life that surprised her. When she was young, her mother always asked her to "Do as I say, not as I do." Her mom was, in Beth's little eyes, above the law. Her mom beat her and punished her and her father just let it happen. He did not agree with her mom on how to discipline the kids, yet at the same time he never supported Beth against her mother's wrath. She wrote her core beliefs to say that "life is unfair" and "no one will ever come to my defense." For the first time, Beth saw the emotional pattern and behaviors those virus-ridden beliefs had created in her life. She realized she had made her boss into her father and the two uncooperative clients into her mother.

Beth met with her boss to discuss the situation. Her boss was aware of what was going on and told her he was behind her 100 percent. All contracts had to be initiated by the cutoff date — period. She realized she perceived the current situation through the eyes of her childhood experiences and reacted to it in that way. She lost all her clarity and ability to think clearly because of her emotional reactions. Beth saw that even if her boss did not support her in obtaining the contracts, there was still no need for her to get upset. Her boss was not her father and it was his business to run the way he wanted and his choice as to whether he would enforce his own rules. It was not a reflection on Beth's ability to do her job, nor was it truth that she would look stupid.

She decided to re-write her core beliefs to read the: "Life will unfold exactly as it unfolds. Only my judgment about it will make it unfair. I understand my expectations about how things should look create my feelings of injustice. I do not need anyone to come to my support or defense. I am not a victim or a child anymore and I will not link my self-worth to whether or not people help me or come to my aid. If I want help or assistance, I have the option of asking for it because I want it and not because I need it."

She saw how her fear-based beliefs were running her life at work and at home and made an effort to watch carefully for whenever she had an emotional reaction to something in her daily life. She was also able to start the forgiveness process toward her parents and forgive herself for perpetuating this pattern in her life. Taking responsibility for this particular behavior pattern, along with letting go of her expectations about how things should function at work, gave her much peace in her daily life. Not taking the actions of co-workers and clients at work to heart gave her emotional state of chronic drama a much-needed rest.

The most important lesson from these two stories is that we rarely see what is happening to us right now for what it is. We're always taking the current situation and filtering it through what we already have in our program (remember Chapter 2?). As a result, our emotional reaction to what is occurring right now doesn't seem appropriate for the situation currently unfolding. This piece of information is your biggest clue – take advantage of this and always ask yourself, "Am I seeing the 'what is' or what I want to see instead."

As a final note, when we start doing work like this, there is a tendency to get angry with ourselves for reacting in situations and for being "so stupid." This is because our awareness is becoming more acute and we are starting to see what we are actually creating in our lives. Please recognize that every situation that you have a reaction to is a huge gift from Spirit to you! Without your emotional reactions you would never recognize the beliefs that are causing you pain in your life. Toltecs never pretend or deny that they are getting upset, but instead embrace their reactions (in an appropriate manner, of course).

### *Some questions for you to consider:*

1. Can you identify several situations in your life now where you have made the current "players" into family members or characters from your past?

2. Can you see how you often perceive what is currently happening in your life through the eyes of old stories and situations?

3. Can you find in the above examples each of the four tools (from chapter 10) that Ralph and Beth used in breaking their fear-based beliefs and agreements?

4. Take one example from your life and practice applying the four tools. I am listing them here for you to make it a little easier!

- Take responsibility for your baggage and not blame it on others.

- Detach from your expectations of what things should look like.

- Stop taking what is happening or being said to heart.

- Forgive yourself and the others involved.

# Chapter 12

## *Identify The Emotions, Find The Beliefs*

**Many times it's difficult to look at** our life situations and determine the beliefs behind them. We can't seem to figure out why we're stuck doing things a certain way. Most of our behavior patterns and virus-ridden beliefs are very well-hidden, buried deep within thousands of files. In this chapter, we're going to look at another method for determining where those corrupt files are so we can root them out and re-write those beliefs. If you spend a little time observing yourself, you will see that for every particular situation, you have a particular emotional reaction, and all of us have our own way of reacting emotionally to life. Your friend has a totally different way of being emotional than you do. It's almost as if each one of us senses differently emotionally or that we have our own emotional signatures. We can call our individual, unique reactions to certain events our emotional template.

If you're not connected to what you're truly feeling, this part of the book will be especially helpful. It's imperative that you become aware of your emotions at all times. So often in workshops people say to me, "I just can't figure out what I am feeling. Can you help me?" Well if you can't figure it out, who can? It can be very scary to determine what you are feeling, and often, it seems easier to avoid the situation. However, chances are you already know what you are feeling; you just don't want to admit it to yourself because of your fear. Fear of what, you might ask? Fear of self-judgment! We react emotionally to a situation and then judge ourselves for having the emotional reaction: "Oh, why did I let my husband see me get upset today? He'll think I am stupid and get aggravated with me even more!" If we pretend not to know what we're feeling, on the other hand, we don't have to judge ourselves. It's often easier to feign ignorance than to admit the truth about our emotions. Remember, this path is about being able to tell the truth, first and foremost to yourself! By going into denial, you're doing yourself a big disservice.

*"Self-pity is easily the most destructive of the non-pharma-ceutical narcotics; it's addictive, gives momentary pleasure and separates the victim from reality."*

— *JOHN W. GARDNER PRESIDENT CARNEGIE FOUNDATION*

### *Ending Mind Spam — Emotions Worksheet*

I've created this worksheet with a list of some of the common fear-based emotions. You can print it out for further reference. You may think of other fear-based emotions you want to add to this list as you become more familiar with what you are feeling. This way the process becomes customized to your own emotional expression or template.

Situation at hand: _____

_____

_____

I feel _____

because I believe _____

_____

_____

| | | | | |
|---|---|---|---|---|
| Abandoned | Defeated | Hatred | Obligated | Self conscious |
| Agitated | Defective | Helpless | Obsessiveness | Self important |
| Alienated | Defensiveness | Hopeless | Overwhelmed | Selfish |
| Anger | Defiant | Humiliated | Pain | Self Pity |
| Angst | Denial | Impatient | Panic stricken | Self rejection |
| Anguish | Depressed | Inadequate | Perfectionism | Separation |
| Annoyed | Desire | Indifferent | Persecuted | Shame |
| Apprehensive | Despair | Inferior | Pride | Shy |
| Anxious | Disgusted | Injustice | Procrastination | Smothered |
| Appalled | Dismay | Insecure | Rage | Stressed |
| Argumentative | Disappointment | Insignificant | Rebellious | Stubborn |
| Betrayed | Doomed | Irresponsible | Rejected | Stupid |
| Bitter | Embarrassed | Irritated | Repulsed | Superior |
| Cheated | Envy | Jealous | Remorse | Tense |
| Competitive | Failure | Lazy | Resentment | Threatened |
| Compulsive | Fear | Lonely | Resistance | Unloved |
| Confused | Foolish | Lustful | Responsible | Vain |
| Contemptuous | Frustrated | Malice | Righteous indignation | Vengeful |
| Controlling | Greedy | Needy | Sad | |
| Cranky | Grief | Numb | Scornful | |
| Craving | Guilty | Nervous | | |

The best way to do this exercise is to make a note of how many times a day you have an emotional reaction. And by that, I don't mean how many times a day you have expressed happiness! We're going to focus on the emotions we experience as a result of fear-based beliefs. So you'll take note of every time you were upset, frustrated, jealous, etc. In doing this, you may find that you're emotional a good part of the day. Again, don't let your denial system hop in and tell you that you weren't really upset or angry, or that you were only momentarily annoyed. If you had an emotional reaction even for a second, it counts, because every time you have react to something based on your fears, you lose energy and give your personal power to the other person involved.

> *If you spend the day happy, you feel great at the end of the day, energized and satisfied. On the other hand, a day of conflict leaves you drained and exhausted. When you get upset, it's like putting your happiness on a beautiful silver platter and handing it over to another person. Why do we want to put other people in charge of our joy? We do this because we can't help ourselves. Situations come up and we automatically react. This is why it's imperative for us to identify our fear-based beliefs. Once identified, they can be re-written and our personal power re-deployed into healthier beliefs. As a result, we're capable of being in control of how we react to things in life and we can choose not to be angry, jealous, or resentful. Instead we can choose happiness.*

Ok, let's say you made a list of every time you got upset today. Now, for each situation listed, see how many of the emotions listed on the worksheet you can identify with. Be as honest as possible! Now take each emotion you checked off and create a sentence that begins in the following way:

"I was feeling (which emotion?) _____
because I believe (what do you believe?) _____."

*For example:* "I was feeling ***ANGRY*** with my girlfriend because I believe she never listens to my problems. I'm always there to help her out, but when it comes to my problems, she blows me off," or, "I was feeling ***RIGHTEOUS INDIGNATION*** toward my mom because I believe she's wrong to be siding with my brother when she knows that he's just using her."

Do this for each emotion you checked off. Once you have a sentence or two for each emotion, it's up to you to see whether those beliefs are bringing you happiness. Look deeply into what you believe and question everything! Identify each belief as either a simple one that can be easily changed or a core belief that will take some work and dedication to re-write. (Simple and core beliefs are discussed in detail in Chapter 7.)

While our emotional reactions are real, the reasons we're experiencing those emotions may not be real. We get upset and react to things that we believe should be a certain way and are not going according to our point of view and our programming. (Expectations again!) When we're in resistance to life, it causes friction and pain and increases our emotional reaction to any situation we're in.

Now let's look at a few examples illustrating how these concepts all work together:

### SITUATION #1
Frank makes a proposal to his boss for a plan of action and his boss vetoes his suggestion. It's not the first time this has happened. Frank lists each emotion he felt in the situation and then writes a sentence or two clarifying why he felt that particular emotion:

"I was feeling ***ANGRY*** with my boss because I believe he never listens to my proposals. I believe he should listen to my proposals because the methods I've suggested are the fastest way to complete the project and I have more experience than most of the other people on the team."

"I was feeling **FRUSTRATED** because I believe my boss purposely ignores my proposals. I keep trying to re-word things so he can see I'm right, but it doesn't help. I can't seem to make him hear me."

"I was feeling **FEAR** because I believe my boss doesn't like me and I could get fired."

"I was feeling **SELF-PITY** because I believe the boss has it out for me. I feel victimized by him."

"I was feeling **REJECTED** by my boss because I believe he doesn't appreciate me, like me, or take my suggestions seriously."

"I was feeling **DEFENSIVE** toward my boss because I believe he is against me so I need to protect myself from him."

"I was feeling **IMPATIENT** with my boss because I believe he's not listening to me. I want to make this project proposal happen and I want him to acknowledge me now."

"I was feeling **NOT GOOD ENOUGH** and **HUMILIATED** by my boss because I believe he's in a position of power over me and he uses it to try to make me feel small and keep me in my place."

"I was feeling **DISAPPOINTED** because I believe no matter how hard I try, my boss will never acknowledge me."

"I was feeling **STUBBORN** because I believe I have to keep showing my boss that my proposals are good and right until he is able to recognize this for himself."

"I was feeling **RESISTANCE** toward my boss because I believe I need to fight him to be heard."

"I was feeling **RESENTMENT** toward my boss because I believe I've been treated badly repetitively. I'm not taken seriously or respected and I'm holding that against him."

"I was feeling **RIGHTEOUS INDIGNATION** toward my boss because I believe I'm right in these situations and he's not."

"I was feeling **COMPETITIVE** because I believe my boss is scared of me taking his place and that's why he doesn't want to acknowledge my good ideas."

"I was feeling **HOPELESS** because I believe the situation will never get better at work."

### SITUATION #2

Here is a scenario where Mary and Annie, have decided that the study in their home needs to be painted, but each has a different idea about when the project should be completed. They have been invited to a pool party. Mary goes; Annie stays home and paints. Annie's feelings on the matter follow:

"I was feeling **RIGHTEOUS INDIGNATION** toward my partner because I believe she was absolutely wrong to leave me alone with this work. She should have offered to help me paint the study rather than going out when she knew I needed her assistance and she promised to help."

"I was feeling **ANGRY** toward Mary because I believe she should be considerate toward my needs and not stick me with all the work."

"I was feeling **REJECTED** because I believe that Mary should not leave me to be with people who should be less important to her than I am."

"I was feeling **ENVIOUS** of Mary because I believe she is more popular with our friends and they don't care if I'm not at the party. I envy her ability to just take off and do fun things when there's work to be done."

"I was feeling **SELF-PITY** because I believe Mary doesn't really love me and that she loves our friends more."

"I was feeling **BETRAYED** because I believe Mary chose our friends over me and she left me to do all the work."

"I was feeling **CONTROLLING** toward my partner because I believe she should have stayed home with me and I want her to feel guilty for leaving me."

"I was feeling **RESENTMENT** because I believe Mary always sticks me with the work around the house and goes to have fun without thinking of how I feel."

"I was feeling **SELFISH** and **NEEDY** because I believe my needs should come first if my partner really loves me."

"I was feeling **FRUSTRATED** with Mary because I believe that she does this purposely over and over again to get me upset and jealous."

"I was feeling **OBSESSIVE** because I believe things should be done when they need to be done."

### SITUATION #3
In this situation, Barbara's perceived fears of her husband's infidelity have been confirmed. When she's able to calmly evaluate her emotions, she writes:

"I was feeling **ANGRY** because I believe I should have known this was going on sooner. I'm so mad at myself for being stupid and unaware. I'm furious with him for doing this to me and subjecting me to this scandal."

"I was feeling **BETRAYED** by my husband because I believe he shouldn't have cheated on me or lied to me. We made a commitment to be together forever, through the good and bad times."

"I was feeling **ABANDONED** and **REJECTED** by my husband because I believe the other woman is younger, prettier, and sexier than me."

"I was feeling **DEPRESSED** and **SADDENED** because I believe our marriage is over and I wasted so many good years of my life in this relationship."

"I was feeling **NOT GOOD ENOUGH** because I believe I can never be as attractive as the other woman or keep up with her."

"I was feeling **HUMILIATED** because I believe everyone knew about this but me and I'm mortified to be around people in our social circle."

"I was feeling **PAIN** because I believe it's so hard to let this relationship go. We have been together so long and this separation and the finality of it all hurts so badly."

"I was feeling **NEEDY** because I believe it's going to be so hard to be without him. I don't want to be alone in my life. I'm nothing without him."

"I was feeling **SELF-PITY** because I believe I am the victim of circumstances here. He cheated on me and I'm the one that has to pay for it."

"I was feeling **FEAR** because I believe it's too scary to be single in these times and no one's going to want me at my age."

"I was feeling **VENGEFUL** because I believe my husband should suffer as much as I have. I'll find a way to get back at him — and at her, because she is a home-wrecker. They'll be sorry they ever did this to me."

"I was feeling **GRIEF** and **ANGUISH** because I believe our relationship is dead and I can't believe this could happen to me. I feel like my life has ended."

"I was feeling **RIGHTEOUS INDIGNATION** towards my husband because I believe he is dead wrong and should know that she can never be as good a partner as me. He has no idea what a terrible mistake he's made; she'll probably dump him in a year and then he'll be sorry."

"I was feeling **REMORSE** and **GUILT** because I believe I did things that drove my husband away from me. I think if I did things differently he might never have left me for her."

"I was feeling **DEFENSIVE** towards my husband because I believe it's him against me now and I have to get all I can from the divorce settlement."

### *Action list to support the practice of using our emotions to detect virus-ridden beliefs:*

#### *Do the exercise:*
Take time now to create some emotion – belief sentences before we advance to the next chapter. I found the easiest way for me to do this was to transfer this list into my computer and print out multiple emotion sheets that I could keep using for each different situation I found myself in. You can punch holes in these sheets and keep them neatly in a binder for future reference.

*Explore a life experience:*

Pick one simple situation in your life where you became emotional and went into reaction. Check off all the fear-based emotions on the list included in this chapter that applied in that situation (and add any that aren't currently on the list). Complete the process in your journal by figuring out the fear-based belief associated with each particular emotion. You may, for example, feel as though you were betrayed in a situation. That belief would reflect your expectations about a particular human concept (like a friendship, a marriage, or trust). So if you told a friend a secret and he turned around and blabbed it to someone else, you might write: "I felt betrayed by Ed because he told Fortunata a personal piece of information that I asked him specifically not to share. I believe my friends should not gossip and talk behind my back; that's just not right."

*Find a supportive friend:*

If you can't think of the corresponding beliefs attached to your emotions, then engage a friend who's also doing this work to assist you. It's often easier for another person to see the belief if you're still emotionally invested in a situation. After all, our emotions make it difficult to have clarity! Don't worry if you can't figure it out at first. This will become easier as you go along. (And in the next chapter, we will be going deeper into this process, so this is just a warm-up exercise for us.)

# Section 4

## *Healing, Repairing, And Rewriting Your Damaged And Corrupted Files*

*"One word frees us of all the weight and pain of life: that word is love."*

— SOPHOCLES

***Once we can clearly see*** the fear-based beliefs that are causing us harm, we have to have a way to get rid of them, or to at least repair them, which is what we'll talk about in Section 4.

Learning to forgive is huge — and we're not talking about just forgiving others. Forgiving ourselves is a vital part of rewriting damaged files, and it starts with acknowledging what we need to forgive ourselves for. Through the act of recapitulation (reviewing one's life), we begin to take stock of what's really happened to bring us to the point we're at now, and we can let go of all the hurt and pain that we've carried with us through the years.

# Chapter 13

## *Recapitulation In Action*

*We discussed truth earlier in this book* and we know that our own truth is just one particular point of view. For our reality to change, we need to let go of our point of view and be able to see any and all possible points of view, something that most of us have never been taught to do. We all know it's important to walk a mile in someone else's shoes, but how often do we make the effort to do so? And even then, we're only looking at one other point of view. It's important to strive to see as many points of view as we can imagine to make it clear to ourselves that we're rarely "right" about anything.

When we're able to do this, we can detach from having to be right, from arguing with others, and from being locked into seeing only one way of thinking. It gives us freedom to figure out different solutions to our problems that we might not normally see. Our whole universe shifts as we invite additional and various possibilities into our lives. Problems turn into challenges, and unsolvable situations blossom into a myriad of opportunities! Remember, the universe works on the basis of action-reaction. If we always take the same actions, we will always get the same reactions. Shifting our point of view will expand our world and create reactions that are new, exciting, and diverse. In this chapter, we're going to revisit the scenarios presented in Chapter 12, this time from a more enlightened point of view.

We'll start with the first scenario involving Frank, who had made a proposal which was rejected by his boss. Frank made a list of the emotions he was feeling and the beliefs he had regarding his situation. He can only express his own point of view and feelings according to his own truth. But we will see that truth is not necessarily the truth.

> "If there is any one secret of success, it lies in the ability to get the other person's point of view and see things from that person's angle as well as from your own."
>
> — HENRY FORD

Frank feels that his proposals are the fastest way to complete the project and that he has more experience than most of the other people he works with. Although one particular method may be the fastest, it does not mean that it's the best way. Also, being experienced does not necessarily mean you know what you are doing in every situation. Frank has not validated anyone else's point of view, nor has he shown his ability to work with others' suggestions, as he hasn't even considered them. Frank keeps re-wording his proposals but his boss still can't see that he's right. Of course, if we're trying to be right then we have to make someone else wrong. Since no one wants to be wrong, Frank's boss is not likely to acknowledge his point of view. Why should he let his employee make him wrong at his own expense?

On his boss's side, Frank has no idea what is happening in the business from his boss's point of view. Because of this, his boss may be behaving in ways that Frank is taking personally when indeed his rejection of Frank's work may be due to completely different and unknown factors. Frank is also scared he could get fired because his boss doesn't like him. It may be true that he could get fired, but it also could be true that he might be responsible for his own firing due to his confrontational behavior.

If Frank feels his boss has it out for him, he must ask himself honestly if he has it out for his boss. It would also be prudent of him to see if indeed he's been responsible for behavior that actually would make his boss want to target him. If he feels victimized it's because he has victimized himself and not because of his boss. Frank is totally unaware of how others perceive him or the way he is behaving. He keeps trying to repeat the same actions at work and can't understand why nothing seems to change. He never takes full responsibility for what he's created, nor has he taken the time to perceive the work situation and dynamics from other possible points of view.

By writing his emotions and beliefs down in a journal, Frank was shocked to see how much he sounded like a victimized child and how stubborn he's been in defending his point of view. Frank thought about the other times in life he'd felt these emotions. Through the process of recapitulation — the act of reviewing one's life story — Frank realized that while he was growing up, he had always been fighting to be acknowledged in his home. His parents never listened to him because they had severe problems going on in their lives that Frank was totally not aware of as a child. In their impatience, they often punished Frank without hearing his side of the story and he always felt that life was unfair. Young Frank just wanted his elders to see that he was right; he knew that if they would just listen to him, they would understand what had really happened, whether it was a question of who broke the window or who ate the last cookie.

> *The act of recapitulation is the process of reviewing your life for the purpose of searching and seeking out all your repetitive behavior patterns that originate from your fear-based beliefs and agreements. By doing this we gain clarity about ourselves and our actions and gain a deeper understanding of why we've taken the actions we have in our lives. With this information we can begin to change our actions to ones that create beauty and happiness, rather than ones that support our corrupted beliefs.*

By reviewing his life in this manner, Frank realized that he has been fighting against authority ever since his childhood days and has turned life into a constant battle; as a result, he has created the very situations he was trying to avoid. His core beliefs read, "Life is unfair and unjust, and I have to fight to get what I need or want," "I am invisible and unimportant," and "If I am perfect I will be lovable," and have been the driving force behind these repetitive emotional reactions and behaviors in his life. After seeing this so clearly, he was able to totally change his perception of what was happening at work and change his relationship with his boss and co-workers. Frank saw how other people at work wanted to share his ideas, not be dominated by them, and that his beliefs were not the absolute truth. By taking the time to communicate with other employees, he came to realize that there were situations at play in the business that he had no idea about. This affected the way his boss was required to address all proposals, not just Frank's. The pressure on his boss from upper management also precipitated much of his boss's recalcitrant behavior and it had nothing to do with Frank at all.

Once Frank saw the lies behind his beliefs, he was able to shift his point of view almost effortlessly. He no longer had to act like a needy child at work or in his personal relationships. Frank rewrote his beliefs to say, "Life can be challenging, but only I can judge it to be just or unjust. I choose to believe that life is perfect as it is and I don't need to fight life anymore. I'm smart, creative, and innovative and I don't need to prove myself to anyone. I do the best I can in any situation, and that's enough. I am lovable just the way I am!"

After Frank saw the truth of his situation, he was able to move on to the next part of the process, which is to forgive. He completed the process by forgiving his parents for passing these virus-ridden beliefs onto him. He realized that his parents did the best they could to raise him and that they didn't mean for their actions to be harmful to him, nor was it their intention to infect his self-worth files. Frank saw they had their own issues and he did not have the awareness as a child to understand them. Frank also saw that he had been harboring a lot of anger and resentment towards his parents from his childhood years and it had been causing him to be argumentative towards them even now. It was time to let all that go and change his actions towards his parents so he could have a beautiful relationship with them in the time they had left together.

Frank also forgave himself for behaving so stubbornly and for always making the people around him wrong. This was the hardest part, since he felt horrible once he saw what he had created in his life. It actually made him ill to think about his past behavior, but he finally let it go and made the decision to forgive his transgressions because he loved himself so much. It helped for him to acknowledge and have gratitude for the fact that his past has gotten him to where he is now, and rather than getting upset about it. Frank went out of his way to apologize to the people in his life he had hurt, including his co-workers. Having compassion for himself allowed him to have more compassion and appreciation for his co-workers and his boss. Having clarity on just this pattern alone changed the way he perceives his life and his overall level of happiness. His forgiveness and newfound awareness was a gift he was able to give himself as an expression of his growing self-love and appreciation. Frank has vowed to continue to scan himself daily until every one of his emotional patterns and reactive behaviors has been discovered and he totally owns his happiness and freedom.

> *Old programming and virus-infected beliefs can no longer hold any sway over you once you see the non-reality of them. This is the entire purpose of recapitulating your life. Eventually, the structure of your life will start to slowly unravel and you will find you no longer react to situations; instead, you just evaluate each event as it happens and take appropriate action. This leads to peace, happiness, and a whole lot of emotional calmness in your life. You will have the clarity to make healthy, life-enhancing choices, and you will never have to depend on others to make choices for you. That's what I call personal power!*

Let's dissect the second scenario from Chapter 12 now. Mary and Annie have decided that the study in their home needs to be painted, but they have different ideas about when the project should be completed. They've been invited to a pool party and while

Mary goes, Annie stays home and paints. Annie feels that Mary is absolutely wrong to leave her home and that if they decide to do a project together, Mary should keep her promise. She feels Mary is inconsiderate of her needs and cares about everyone else more. She's envious of Mary's popularity with their friends and her ability to have fun, yet she makes no effort to transform those aspects within herself. She believes that work needs to be completed before play and that if Mary loved her she would prove it by helping her paint.

When Annie puts her emotions and beliefs in her journal, she's surprised to see how at the mercy of her partner she seems to be. It immediately reminds her of how her father used to always make excuses to get out of the house on weekends in order to get away from her mother. Annie's mom used to become infuriated when he went out and played golf and left her with the responsibility of the children and household. She held that over her husband's head and used it to manipulate him. Little Annie observed this behavior and saw that manipulation is the way people get what they want. Annie downloaded the following virus-ridden beliefs from her mother and father: "The people you love hurt you," "Life is suffering and pain," and "Life is unfair." She can see how similar her emotions toward Mary are to what her mom felt toward her father.

The thought that she has been reliving her parent's life in her own relationship is particularly upsetting to Annie. She always told herself she'd never be like her mom, but here she is, a mirror image of her! Upon recapitulating her childhood and making this realization, she makes a promise to stop using manipulation to get what she wants from her partner and instead to use clean, clear communication based in her love for Mary. She realizes that the world won't not end if chores get put off for a weekend and that her social life will seriously improve (along with her level of joy) if she lets go of her belief that chores need to be done in a certain time frame. This will allow her to spend more quality time with Mary and her friends.

Annie also realizes that Mary will be more willing to participate in these chores and projects when she doesn't feel like she is being manipulated. Annie decides to re-write her beliefs to say, "The only suffering and pain in my life comes from my adherence to my rigid beliefs, having to be right, and the attachment to my expectations about what everything should look like. I believe life is beautiful and filled with joy and I will be flexible no matter what life brings me. Life is only unfair when I judge it to be that way or create it in that way. The people in my life don't hurt me. My expectations and my need to take their actions personally are what create my pain."

Annie then took the time to sit with herself and make a list of everyone she needed to forgive in this situation and who she wanted to ask forgiveness of. She realized that she's always perceived her mom as a martyr, which has made it difficult to be around her. In seeing that her behavior is exactly the same as her mom's, she vows to forgive her mom and have compassion for her situation. She sees that her mom did not have the awareness to see her own patterns in life and did the best she could, given her own domestication. Annie also wants to forgive her father for participating in that pattern and perpetuating it for all those years. She also spends some time with Mary sharing what she has learned about herself and her past and asks Mary to forgive her for her manipulative behavior. Lastly, Annie works on forgiving herself for martyring herself, for controlling and manipulating others, and for treating her mom so harshly.

Situation 3 from Chapter 12 is very common, one that many of us have experienced in some variation. Barbara's fears of her husband's infidelity have been confirmed. She feels so many emotions going through her at the same time, she can hardly write them all down. She's angry at her husband, as if everything that has happened is his fault. He is the one who has destroyed the marriage and she's the good wife. She's furious with the "witch" who stole her husband, as if he were the victim of her wily seduction! Barbara blames her husband for not honoring their marriage vows and for embarrassing her in their social circle. She also feels guilty for all the times she argued with her husband, thinking that perhaps these things caused him to have an affair. Or maybe, she thinks, she didn't satisfy him in bed or she is just getting too old to interest him anymore. She's also scared to be alone or to change her lifestyle after all these years. Her fear makes her doubt her ability to survive without her husband and she feels like she'll be nothing without him.

With the help of a dear friend, Barbara sits down to honestly look at what she believes about her situation. She sees how emotional she is and is struck by how all of the beliefs she listed are based in fear, not love. It amazes her that what she believes about her situation is causing her pain and feelings of victimization, rather than the situation itself! Yes, she realizes she is grieving for her lost relationship and the love she once had for her husband, but the truth is that she hasn't loved him for many years. In fact, she has been living a lie for years just to avoid facing her fears of leaving and being alone. It was difficult for her to admit this to herself, since she believed that her marriage would last forever.

In making a list in her journal, Barbara discovers some disturbing beliefs: "I believe women can't be trusted and that they want to steal my husband," "I'm nothing without a man," "I can't make it on my own without a man and his income," "I'm not worth loving," " I won't be welcome as a single woman in my social circle because the other women will be suspicious of me," "I'm old and ugly and not progressive sexually," "Marriage should be 'till death do we part,'" "You should stay with your husband until the children are totally grown," "It's wrong to have an affair when you're married," "If your husband cheats on you, get a good lawyer and take him for all he is worth." She's horrified that she actually could be so petty and self-centered!

Barbara starts to look over her life and sees that although her husband definitely has his own problems, half of the problems in the marriage were created by her own expectations, demands, and issues. She sees that her constant nagging, based on her thousands of simple beliefs, acted like thorns in her husband's side. In retrospect, Barbara could see that all the beliefs that she put her faith into were not worth the breakup of her marriage. She could see that her lack of self-love was what was making her want to be with a husband who did not really love her anymore.

She decided to re-write her beliefs and to start to change the way she perceived herself and her life. Barbara journaled the following new beliefs: "I believe women are amazing and resourceful. I'm not afraid of them, nor do I believe anyone can 'steal' another person from a relationship. I'm complete all by myself and don't need a man to be whole. I don't need to depend on anyone for my financial freedom. Spirit has given me many talents and I can use them in many directions. I'm blessed with wonderful friends and family. I'm beautiful just the way I am and I can express myself sexually with a partner who wants to be with me."

She also decided that "Children relate better to two parents that love each other separately than to parents that hate each other in proximity. I no longer desire to make others wrong and myself right. I no longer desire to seek revenge because I no longer am a victim of my life. I want to make sure my children are financially cared for and their needs covered. I am happy to negotiate for a fair settlement of what we have worked hard for together."

It took Barbara a while to work through all of her beliefs before she was finally able to get to the point where she could forgive herself for her responsibility in the demise of the relationship. She realized she didn't have awareness of what she was doing and didn't have the ability to see how her beliefs were running her life. In taking total responsibility for her half of the marriage, she was also able to forgive her husband's weakness, fear, and inability to admit that that he was discontented with their relationship and having an affair. Barbara was finally able to stop taking her husband's actions to heart and be free of placing the burden of the demise of the relationship upon herself.

She also spent time recapitulating her life and discovering the origins of her beliefs. A lot of them came from what she was taught when she was young and spent some time forgiving her grandmother and mom for those beliefs. Some of the more important false beliefs like; "I must stay in my marriage even if it's no longer loving just because of the children," "Marriage is a forever commitment" and "A woman alone is a failure" were challenged. She realized that these old societal beliefs were not supporting her in a loving way, and were creating great limitation in her life.

In the end, Barbara used the divorce as an opportunity to teach her children what she had learned about love and forgiveness and that their father did not take that action to hurt or embarrass them. Barbara asked the kids for forgiveness, too. In this way, she strengthened her relationship with them and what could have been a devastating time for the family ended up being an incredible opportunity for self-growth and self-love. Barbara learned that a breakup can be what ever you make it to be. Who says it must look like a TV soap opera?

### *Action list to support the practice of recapitulation:*

#### *Reflect on your life:*
Take some time to look at several situations that are happening right now in your life and see if you can comprehend how you are viewing what is occurring currently through the eyes of your programmed past? Can you relate these scenarios with behavior patterns and beliefs that have their origin in your childhood?

# Chapter 14

## *A Viral Scan A Day Keeps Corruption Away*

"To see clearly is poetry, prophecy and religion - all in one."

— *JOHN RUSKIN*

***Once you've taken inventory*** of your emotions and beliefs and quarantined the infecting viruses in your corrupted system files, you'll be well on your way to a cleaner and healthier mind. And by the time you've healed the damage the viruses created in your program by re-writing and replacing your virus-ridden beliefs you'll really be seeing a difference in your life!

As we discussed earlier in the book, it's beneficial to have a written record of your work — a journal — because you can always refer back to it years down the line and appreciate how far you've come.

At first it's a bit confusing to actually look at your beliefs and decide whether they're the truth or not. After all, if you didn't think they were the truth, you wouldn't have believed them in the first place, right? This is the whole predicament in a nutshell! We need to re-examine everything we have come to hold sacred and challenge its validity. The best way to do this is to ask the question, "Is this belief coming from the fear of not having something I think I need to survive?" Simply put, fear-based beliefs cause us to have fear-based emotions.

---

*You must be ruthless (meaning, you must have no pity) with yourself when examining your beliefs. We've already discussed the power of the denial system and its desire to keep us from seeing the truth and becoming free. Our beliefs seem so logical and reasonable to us, how can they not be true? As we also discussed earlier in the book, our beliefs are centered on concepts that humans have created — but just because we created them does not mean they're true! It takes absolute courage to let go of the very concepts we have based our lives on and put our faith in so blindly in for so many years.*

---

Now let's spend a little more time talking about combining the processes of recapitulation, forgiveness, and letting go. Each of us feels like we know exactly how to do what we need to do and the way everything should look in our lives. The problem here is that this "knowing" is a direct reflection of the point of view of our program, which keeps us locked into doing things exactly the same way, over and over again. As a result, change is very challenging for us. We keep taking actions that seem to be different to us, but are in fact actions that only have the tiniest of variations from that which we normally do. These patterns of "doings" have been slowly reinforced and cultivated over many years. By recapitulating our lives, we gain clarity about these patterns, where they began, and which emotional needs they were created to satisfy. Herein lies the beauty of following your emotional reactions backward through your life. They will lead you directly to the agreements and beliefs you have that are hurting and limiting you in your adult life.

As adults, we have the power to evaluate whether or not a particular emotional pattern and its associated beliefs are currently useful for our survival or if they are even healthy for us. In the previous chapter, we read about people having emotional reactions based not on what was happening in the moment, but instead on aspects of the current situation that reminded them subconsciously of old beliefs and agreements they made to totally different situations. The critical issue here is that we can't possibly be taking affirmative action right now nor can we have the clarity to make healthy choices if we perceive our current situations as if they were events that happened years ago.

To be free of our fear-based beliefs, we need to regain the ability to take action in response to what is currently occurring in our lives, unaffected by our past experiences, fears and judgments. This is truly living life in the moment. Most humans have no concept what it's like to be totally present right now, making choices not based on future worries or past concerns. I encourage you to carefully look at each of the lists of emotions and corresponding beliefs that you've created. There is gold in each of them that will lead you to greater self-knowledge and self-empowerment. Only you have the power to decide what happened in your past — not from the point of view you currently hold regarding all past events but from the larger truth that encompasses all points of view.

The key is to stop looking at your past as an adult remembering what happened back then, and instead become the child or the person you were when you actually experienced that event. I know that many occurrences in your past may be painful to remember, but if you can go back and be the child you were then, witnessing what happened, thinking like a child instead of an adult, this will help create enough emotional detachment to allow you to revisit what happened with clarity. In doing this, you will find that you didn't always interpret things clearly back then because children have a very egocentric view of life: They feel that everything they experience is their fault, or is happening because of them, or that the entire world is revolving around them — and this, of course, is not true.

For example, you may currently have the belief that life is not fair and filled with injustice because of terrible things that happened when you were young, and while those things may have been very traumatic, as a child, you didn't consider the motivations of the people who caused your trauma. You didn't have the ability to perceive things in that way or to have the awareness of other people's points of views. Telling yourself the truth about your life and past means being able to see your entire life with clarity and understand all points of view. This does not, however, mean you have to agree with what happened or think it was great. Absolutely not!

So if you were sexually abused, for example, you don't have to condone that behavior, but you can come to understand that your abuser's motivations had absolutely nothing to do with you personally. Knowing this can totally change the way you perceive yourself. Rather than believing that you are no good or that you will never have love in your life or never be able to trust in love, you can change those beliefs by forgiving the person who abused you — and by forgiving yourself for being in that situation. This last action is absolutely essential. I want to make it clear that as children we did not have the resources to get ourselves out of such traumatic situations, but we don't have to spend our lives blaming ourselves for those events. That is why it's always necessary for us to forgive both the persons who hurt us and ourselves for being there.

> *Most people who do heinous things do so because they believe things that are not truth and these lies empower them to act in evil ways. The key is that they don't realize they believe in lies and that's why they do what they do. This is a very important concept and you may want to meditate on this for a while before continuing on.*

The next step in healing the damage the viruses created in your program is to forgive yourself and the people involved in your current situation, along with those people from the past who gave you those virus-ridden beliefs in the first place. The process of healing your damaged files is not complete without forgiveness. We forgive because we love ourselves, not because we think the other person was right to do what they did. We're all responsible for hurting others or ourselves, whether it was without our awareness or with purpose. Forgiveness is a very special expression of unconditional love. It totally shifts the balance of energy in a situation and it always feels good!

Remember, you can't drag your baggage around your whole life without suffering the consequences of it. Don't be afraid to let go of your resentments and anger. Look at the other person's situation with detachment, compassion, and love. Forgive yourself for using those old beliefs against yourself without awareness. Corrupted files can only live in an environment that supports those beliefs. When you cultivate self-love and self-respect, there is no room for virus-ridden beliefs hiding in corrupt files!

> *You may find that the forgiveness part of this process challenging. Don't be concerned at this time if you are unable to forgive yourself or the other people involved in a particular event. Practice will yield results — if not now, then in the future. I encourage you not to give up hope and to continue taking the action to forgive, regardless of the current results. One day, when you least expect it, you'll be able let go and forgiveness will come to you. Even if you think you could never forgive yourself or another person, anything is possible if you want to heal with all your heart and Spirit. This is the power of Intent in action.*

If you have clearly defined your virus-infected fear-based beliefs then you can use your journal to change those beliefs that you are ready and willing to let go of now. Computer programmers are constantly re-writing and tweaking versions of programs; you can do the same thing as it suits your purpose. You may re-write them as a version you feel you can accept at this time, and then in 6 months, perhaps you will find it's time to re-write those beliefs again in a more expansive form. This is your personal growth and you will do this in your way. Telling the truth about your beliefs means being able to recognize honestly whether you are truly ready to let go of a belief or not. Most importantly, if you are not ready, you owe it to yourself to accept where you are emotionally right now without self-judgment. Otherwise, you are using your spiritual path to abuse yourself and hurt yourself yet again.

You can refer back to the previous chapter for examples of how to re-write your beliefs to be more supportive and life-affirming.

Notice that just writing your belief in a new way does not necessarily mean that you will automatically live your life differently. Your previous behavior followed a pattern for many years, and it will take much attention and awareness on your part to catch yourself engaging in these comfortable self-sabotaging reactions and routines. Remember to have patience with yourself. Children fall down countless times before they finally master the art of walking. Would you yell at, beat up, or berate a child for falling? Of course not! Same thing applies here: You're learning a new skill and for sure, you will fall. But self-love and self-admiration, added to your desire to change your life, will prevent those self-judgments from discouraging you on your path.

By putting your new beliefs into action in your life, you'll be re-programming yourself automatically. If you take different actions in your life, truly different actions, the reactions will also be totally different. This is very exciting! You may find that your program doesn't want to acknowledge the new and wonderful results of your actions because they don't support your old programming. But by transferring your faith into these new beliefs that are creating wonderful results in your life, you will disable and render useless your old beliefs and corrupted programming.

You will find that if you complete the exercises that I've have laid out in the previous chapters and incorporate them into your daily life, your anger, resentments, frustrations, and self-pity won't be able to pile up. You'll live in the moment and resolve your issues daily, rather than dragging them with you from one day to the next. You'll feel happier within a very short time and notice that situations that would normally upset you no longer do so, or if they do, your reaction is short-lived! You won't give your happiness away to others and will develop an acute sense of awareness of the different programs and emotional templates of the people around you. Automatically, you'll become more respectful of others because you'll see their actions and emotional turmoil as a reflection of your own, because you have understanding and compassion for your own emotional processes. As a result, it will become easier for you to communicate with others, your energy level will increase, and you'll actually enjoy your day.

In scanning yourself each day, you'll catch any viruses you may have missed. Sometimes, you'll find these virus-ridden beliefs in one file and think you have quarantined them, but then they reappear in another file, worded slightly differently. This gives them a chance to re-assert themselves and make trouble for you again. But with awareness, you can say, "Oops, there it is again. I thought I had it, but here I am working on the same thing from a different angle!" This is normal. You have thousands and thousands of files and the process of scanning and correcting all of them may take some years to complete. (After all, it took years to form all these files, so have patience when it comes to dismantling them.) And who cares how long it takes?

Don't let your program tell you if you can't do it in a week, it's not worth doing! The point is that you are doing something now to make a difference in your life. Understand that until you're tested in a real-life situation, you may never know if you've totally quarantined and re-written your beliefs. You'll know you've healed yourself of those viruses when you no longer have an emotional response like you used to in a given situation — instead, you just take action and do what you need to. No drama, no whining, no worrying, and no complaining! That's why every situation in life is another opportunity for growth and change, if you allow it to be.

> *It's best if you can put aside some time every evening to do the scanning process, but if your schedule doesn't allow for this, there are other opportunities throughout the day. You may ride the train, drive a car, or walk someplace daily. Maybe you have a few minutes alone in the bathroom in the morning, or some time on your lunch break, or while riding the stationary bike at the gym. Prioritize your time and remove any and all routines that aren't absolutely necessary, making some room in your life for you. With practice this process will become easy. Remember, it's not about "perfection" and there is no "right" way of doing this. Don't use this as an excuse to say you can't do this work or to beat yourself up again.*

Learn to look at every situation in life as a challenge, so to speak. If you react differently than you used to, if you can handle a situation with grace and love rather than frustration and rancor, you know you've succeeded. At the beginning of my spiritual path, I would get so excited when I didn't react to situations that would normally push my buttons. Now I can't even imagine how I survived such a roller coaster of emotions. I love the peace and joy that has descended on my life, the awareness of the magic of life, and the quiet perfection of every moment. You can have this too if you're willing to make the investment in yourself.

Think about this: How much money have you wasted on clothes that are still hanging with tags in your closet? Or how many electronic "toys" have you purchased that are just sitting in the garage? How much time have you whiled away doing nothing? We invest time and money on many things that will never bring us true happiness, just the temporary illusion of it. Look at what you have and invest a portion of your resources into your own life. I've spent about the same amount of money on my personal growth as on my medical education, and it's been the best money I've spent in my entire life, as well as the best investment I've ever made in myself. What monetary value can you put on your self-worth? What is the true value of one life? These are questions that only you can answer for yourself. Again, this is just another awareness exercise for you to gain more clarity about yourself and your programming.

The only way this or any process can work is if you take action. I know I've mentioned this before, but unless your desire for your personal freedom is the Number 1 priority in your life, you can never expect your results to be anything but a reflection of the effort you put out. I've seen thousands of fair-weather spiritual warriors. When they feel like they have the time, the money, and the energy, they do the work. When times are more challenging, though, they say they can't concentrate on themselves because other things are more important. If you want a life filled with love and joy, you have to create that for yourself. No one is going to give it to you — not even a teacher, guide, or guru. When you say that you're too busy to work on yourself, what you're really saying is everything and everyone else in your life is more important than you! Do you really want to be a martyr in that way?

When I was practicing medicine in Florida, many of my patients were over 70 years old, and some were over 100. The one thing they cautioned me about was that life goes by way too fast and before you know it, you're aging, sick, or prematurely dead. Follow your dreams, they said, before it's too late. Our dilemma is that when we're young, we feel like we have forever to accomplish our goals. We forget that we're in the process of dying from the moment we're born. If you only had a day to live, what would your priorities be? I feel there is only one game in town, and that is one's transformation, one's happiness, and one's personal freedom.

Some of you may perceive this as selfishness, but it's actually the opposite. If you give up your life for others and feel resentment as a result, that's true selfishness and self-importance, because you're martyring yourself to look good in the eyes of others. By taking care of yourself and loving yourself first, you will automatically uplift everyone around you as a result of your happiness. Now that is self-love and selflessness! Basically anything other than your personal freedom is just a pleasant or not-so-pleasant diversion. Believe me, I understand how your attention can be easily hooked by the illusions around you, but you are totally in charge of your choices. Choose life, choose love, and choose you! Walk your path and fill your journey with as much love, joy and happiness that you can possibly bear and share it wherever you go.

> *I'm a proponent of marking important affirmations and changes in life with some kind of ceremony. While doing this work, please consider doing something for yourself to celebrate the changes you are making on your path. The purpose is to reward yourself for your bravery and for doing your best to make a difference in your own life. This can be something a simple as lighting a candle in your home to mark your transition and to acknowledge the commitment to your new love-based belief or your decision to forgive something critical from your past. Whatever you choose to do, make it something meaningful for you that represents the commitment you have made to your personal freedom. This is part of the practice of loving yourself, acknowledging yourself, and respecting yourself — actions we tend to run short of in our daily lives.*

*Action steps to begin the viral scan:*

Each day, take note of all the times you registered a fear-based emotional reaction to someone's words or actions, or to something that has transpired. In other words, how many times were your "buttons pushed" today? It would be best to start with the major emotional events of the day and then, after you get the hang of this process, add the smaller emotional reactions. For example, you may have had a major emotional reaction to your significant other today, but also you may have become upset when you had to wait in a slow line in the grocery store. In both situations, you were emotionally tweaked, but the emotional reaction to your beloved has a greater impact on your life than your reaction in the grocery store. It's a matter of prioritizing what you put your attention on, especially if you are unable to dedicate a lot of time to this process at first. In summary, I have listed the process step-by-step for you:

1. List or check off all the fear-based emotions that you are feeling in whatever situations you choose to work with.

2. Create a sentence with each applicable emotion that goes like this: I am feeling _____ with _____ because I believe _____ . List all your beliefs around each emotion checked.

3. Look at the list of your feelings and ask yourself when you have felt this pattern or set of emotions before. Can you identify which situations in your past this current situation reminds you of emotionally? Recapitulate from the present to as far back into your childhood as you can.

4. Journal any and all realizations you've made about yourself from this recapitulation.

5. Evaluate all the beliefs you've listed. Is there any truth to them at all? How many are based in fear rather than love? Remember, we don't have fear-based emotional reactions to beliefs that come from love or Spiritual truth.

6. Re-write the beliefs that you have identified as being fear-based that you are willing to change at this time.

7. Forgive yourself and anyone else you need to in relation to this particular situation. You can write your affirmation of forgiveness in your journal to document it.

8. Light a candle or create a small ceremony to express your compassion, love, and appreciation for yourself for letting go of what is no longer serving the highest expression of yourself.

# Section 5

## *Upgrading The Program*

*"The moment one definitely commits oneself, then providence moves too. All sorts of wonderful things occur to help one that would never otherwise have occurred. A whole stream of events issues from the decision, raising in one's favor all manner of unforeseen incidents and meetings and material assistance which no man could have dreamed would come his way. Whatever you can do or dream, you can begin it. Boldness has genius, power, and magic in it. Begin it now."*

— *GOETHE*

**There are many tools** to assist you in creating a program that will support love-based rather than fear-based beliefs. By doing this you will be optimizing the speed and efficiency of your program in so many ways; not only that, you'll be happy — what a concept! If you inventory all your beliefs, quarantine all the viruses, and rewrite the damaged files, you won't get caught up in useless emotional reactions and fear-based behaviors that drain your personal power. You won't have to fight hidden system files that want to sabotage your relationships or ability to create a successful business life. You will no longer have to deal with conflicting belief files that make it difficult to make choices and decisions. Needing to defend your point of view and participate in arguments will be a thing of the past.

In each of the following chapters, you'll find tools that you can use everyday, starting right now, in addition to those that you've read about already. These are skills that are easy to practice on a daily basis but will produce profound change. As I've said many times in this book, action is the key. Making new habits and initiating new activities makes all the difference.

# Chapter 15

# *Optimizing Your Program With Respect*

*Self-respect is a beautiful human concept* which is the result of loving ourselves absolutely, not from the point of view of self-importance, but from the place of a deep honoring of ourselves. How do we honor ourselves? Well, by having respect for our beliefs, our bodies, our physical space, and our Spiritual self. When we have respect for ourselves, we have boundaries that others can't cross. In other words, when we truly love ourselves, no one else can abuse us, misuse us, or hurt us. With self-respect, we don't give our personal power to others to use against us. We don't engage in interactions with people that go against ourselves or our integrity. This same respect also extends to all other creatures and living entities on the earth. It's a result of knowing that we're all part of the One and by harming another, we ultimately harm ourselves.

*"When you are content to be simply yourself and don't compare or compete, everybody will respect you."*
— *LAO-TZU*

Our self-importance tells us we deserve respect, but when we feel that others must do exactly what we want when we want it, we're not having respect for other people and their programs. This just creates conflict and more lack of respect. When we treat people as if they are below us, talking to them as though they are stupid children or brainless employees, we're forgetting that all living beings are deserving of kind treatment. Humility borne of the understanding that all life is of equal importance always creates respect. We confuse humility in our society with putting our self below others, but truly it comes from being on par with them. Our own self-importance wants to put us on a pedestal; this will always lead to us putting others below our own level. I am sure you could think of people in your life who you think are worthless. Many factors have come together to create challenges for that person that are not for any of us to judge. It's very important to know in your heart, not in your mind, that everyone is the same. Only in this way can we have true compassion and respect for others.

For example, when we abuse others, it's usually because we have learned that behavior from others during our domestication or that we have been abused ourselves. If you have the eyes of truth, you'll see that the person who treats another with disrespect has no respect for themselves. The most important kind of respect, then, is self-respect. If we have self-respect, we treat others as equals, we don't talk down to people, scream at them, or abuse them. When a person has been made to feel not good enough, they tend to either become meek and powerless or become abusive themselves. So it behooves you to look at your childhood with honesty and see if your current behavior is a reflection of what you learned during your upbringing. Which are you, a doormat or an abuser? Or does your position switch, depending on what situation you are in and with whom?

> *People with self-respect don't stay in relationships that are emotionally or physically abusive. Again, this means having boundaries. Of course the same goes for you — no one has to listen to you spew your garbage at them. Clear communication is a result of healthy self-respect and respect for others.*

Having clear boundaries lets others know how far they can go with you. Just remember that one person's boundary is another's line of freedom. Your program is different from others, so make yourself clear on this point. Of course people will always push the limits — it's their nature to want to get what they want from you — but you don't have to allow it if it goes against you. Self-respect means saying no when you want to say no and saying yes when you want to say yes. That applies in any situation, from your friends asking you to help by being on a committee you have no time for, to wanting to say yes to an exciting new activity your programming is telling you is too scary to participate in.

Another aspect of practicing self-respect is not going against ourselves, something we often do by avoiding actions that we know are necessary to change what's not working for us in our lives. For example, many of us find it difficult to maintain a diet or an exercise program, or to begin a spiritual practice, or to simply get going on something we're not enthusiastic about doing, like cleaning out the garage or closets. All of these things require dedication, discipline, and desire — to ourselves, first and foremost. When we become disciplined and dedicated, we're exercising our will and desire, two important qualities necessary for developing a respectful and creative life.

You may have noticed this pattern in your life played out over the years. Perhaps when you were young, you procrastinated in school and crammed for tests, or could never follow through with things. Maybe you're still doing the exact same thing in other aspects of your life without even realizing it. We've been talking a lot about taking action, but what stops us from doing so is lack of will, desire, dedication, and discipline. For most of us, all of our will and personal power are invested in maintaining our program. In other words, we have no free will available. You will find it easier and easier to be disciplined once you have more personal power freed up as a result of isolating those viruses and letting go of all those beliefs that are corrupt and creating limitation and fear in your life.

If you look at your life carefully, you'll see that you have discipline for doing all the things that steal your energy and make your life tiring. Re-setting priorities in your life will assist you in changing these life-draining habits. Every morning you get up and take a shower, brush your teeth, and do your hair and makeup or shave. That routine is a discipline and if you can manage to do that, you can manage to make time to do a virus scan on yourself every night or to change something in your life you don't like or goes against yourself. Ask yourself, where is your desire when you feel lazy? How much do you want a better and happier life? How much do you want to enjoy your days and not be at the mercy of your program and the emotional turmoil that results from your attachment to your beliefs? How much do you want to quit smoking, drinking, gossiping, partying, overeating, overworking, or whatever it is that's causing harm in your life and to those around you?

> *When we think of failure, failure will be ours. If we remain undecided, nothing will ever change. All we need to do is want to achieve something great and then simply do it. Never think of failure, for what we think will come about.*     — MAHARISHI MAHESH YOGI

We need to engage our will to be able to set our priorities. I hear friends complaining all the time, but they don't take action. They grumble about their weight, how lousy they feel, and how they look fat. If we look at the truth of the situation, a totally different picture emerges. My friends are using the concept of weight to abuse themselves and make it okay to disrespect themselves, to call themselves names, and to judge themselves as being ugly. (Wow! Look at how the program spams us with our full participation.) That's why self-respect is so important! I have absolute self-respect, so I will not use the contents of my program against myself. If I don't get to the gym, I recognize that I simply made a choice not to go; it was not a priority. Why should I insult myself, put myself down, or judge myself to be gross?

Of course, what we're talking about here is creating new, healthy habits that will bring abundance in life — abundance of energy, health, creativity, friends, fun, enthusiasm, joy, and yes, even financial abundance. Look at what's important to you, decide what you desire, and discipline yourself to take action. And if you aren't going to exercise your will to take action, then stop putting yourself down and be happy the way you are. After all, this is the choice you are really making isn't it? If you want to change something, then take action in re-prioritizing your life. And if you can't do this, at least you can stop complaining and getting yourself upset about the things you obviously don't find important enough to change.

Get in the habit of creating a daily action list of things that you will do each day to create more joy and love in your life. For example, you might list the following goals for today:

- I will talk in front of my book club to practice getting over my shyness. (Practicing cultivating will, taking action to rewrite limiting beliefs.)

- I will ask that person out who I have been afraid to talk to in the past. (Practicing self-love and respect.)

- I will not allow myself to argue with my parents when they discuss my children. (Practicing setting boundaries, respect.)

- I will say no when my best friend asks me to help him move. I will not let him take advantage of my friendship and kindness. (Practicing setting boundaries, respect.)

- I will not over-exercise at the gym today. I will just do the best I can. I don't have to lose ten pounds in one week. (Practicing respect of the body.)

- I will spend a few minutes alone tonight before bed setting my Intent and thanking Spirit and myself for this day, no matter how good or bad my program wants to judge me for my performance today. (Practicing self-love, creating the experience of Spirit in your life.)

If you have a Palm Pilot, you can put your action list there so you have it with you all day and you can add to it if necessary. I was never fond of gizmos, so I just make an old fashioned list and take it with me in my bag. It doesn't matter how you make your list as long as you make it and take it. As you move through this process, you'll be able to accomplish so much more in life — it will seem like magic! If your first priority is yourself, you won't let non-important things take your attention and time away.

Whenever we make the commitment to self-awareness we must contend with our habit of self-judgment. One of the kindest ways of expressing self-respect is though the practice of patience, gratitude, grace, and love, first for ourselves and then in the direction of others. We're such an instant gratification society these days. We have instant foods, instant e-mail messages, cell phones, microwaves, faxes, and pagers. Everything has to be right now and not a minute later. As a formerly competitive person, I had an incredibly difficult time having patience with my spiritual path. I wanted to work through my programming and heal myself as if I were going though medical school again. I wanted an A.

Well, I'll tell you straight out it doesn't work like that. Your path will take exactly as long as it will take and that is that. Develop patience in life and your days will be filled with joy instead of frustration. Your desire for things to move quickly will not speed things up, and your expectations about the outcome will only cause upset and pain. This applies not only to your own path, but to waiting on lines at the grocery store and bank, waiting in traffic, waiting at the doctors' office, working with people who are learning slowly, and dealing with children. How many times a day do you lose your patience? (Be honest!)

Gratitude is another gift of self-respect you can give to yourself. By this I mean having gratitude for everything that has happened in your life up to this moment in time. I don't care how horrible you or society may judge your life to be. Without everything that's happened to you, you wouldn't be here today. We only know how things have turned out; we'll never know how they might have been if things had gone differently at any point. There's simply no comparison to make between what is and what might have been. Would I choose to remove all of the traumatic incidences that have occurred in my life if I could? Well sure — who wouldn't? But the truth is that we can't erase the past, so our only choice, if we want to be happy, is to have gratitude! And in order to do this, we must forgive everyone who has ever done harm to us, ourselves included. I have absolute gratitude for everything that has occurred in my life — everything! Freedom depends on letting go of anger, resentments, grudges, frustrations, and hate. There is no way around this, believe me.

Grace is one of those qualities that can seem so elusive, so hard to define, yet it's an absolute necessity for negotiating the turmoil and pain of looking into those dark places in your program. Our journey on the path of life can be graceful, an elegant process. You can have grace for yourself by giving yourself kindness and loveliness along the way. Grace helps keep away that tendency to get down on ourselves when the going gets rough and the road seems so dark. It acts as a light on the road, a reassuring sign. Grace is also a side effect of self-respect and admiration for one's life and accomplishments.

Love is the most important quality on your path, so start taking action to love yourself immediately. Look in the mirror every morning and say, "I love you." Do it over and over again until your head stops telling you that this is a stupid thing to do. That is your program's way of sabotaging yourself with spam and denying yourself love. Set aside one day a week to take a beautiful bath with candles and lovely music or to take yourself to a movie, for a game of golf or out to lunch. Don't be afraid to be alone and present with yourself, and I mean without the TV going or music blasting. If you don't enjoy being alone with yourself, how can you expect anyone else to want to be with you?

We need to learn to love ourselves first, totally and absolutely. If we do, self-respect, gratitude, patience, and forgiveness are gifts we have no problems giving to ourselves. If we love ourselves we have no problems setting boundaries, staying within our integrity, or saying NO! Support your creative nature, your self-growth, and your desire to expand and explore. Stop spamming yourself and stop believing your programming. Love yourself by rewriting the nonsense in your mind and quarantining those viruses. Take action by inviting lovely people into your life and escorting those people who don't support your higher good out of your life.

> *Love yourself by bringing beauty into your life, whether it's a new plant, a sweet pet, a piece of artwork, lovely music, or a new place to live with lots of sunshine. Create rituals for yourself to support your progress. Express your imagination! Maybe this means creating a collage of pictures representing what you would like to create in your life and setting your Intent to continue on your path no matter how things are going. Or perhaps it's a simple prayer or affirmation said with all the love in your heart for continued daily strength and courage. Practice giving your love to others generously rather than doling it out in little bits. It isn't as if you have a limited quantity of love available or that it's possible to deplete the supply.*

If you want unconditional love from others, practice giving it to people in your life without any expectations. That includes your dad, cranky Aunt Frances, and your prickly boss. Maybe you don't want to spend the entire day with your aunt, but you can decide to take her to lunch and give her all your attention and love during that time. If your dad is abusive, you don't need to live at home, but you can choose small amounts of time to be present with him and love him despite his behavior. As a person with awareness, you know that your aunt and father may never change, and that they may be slaves to their rigid programs for the rest of their lives, but they

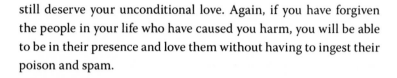

still deserve your unconditional love. Again, if you have forgiven the people in your life who have caused you harm, you will be able to be in their presence and love them without having to ingest their poison and spam.

### *Action list to support the practice of self-respect within you:*

#### *Respect your body and your mind:*
If you work yourself to exhaustion, exercise too much in the war to stay thin, or put foods in your body that go against yourself, create new habits that support your physical body. If your home is a disorganized mess, make it a more pleasant space to relax in. And now that you know a program is running your mind, have respect for that program. Stop spamming and beating yourself up for every mistake and error you make. Have compassion for the mind that got you where you are today, for better or for worse. Use your mind's computer to the best of its abilities and understand its limitations, for there are some things that are beyond the capabilities of the rational mind and reside solely in the realm of the heart.

#### *Respect others:*
Treat your co-workers and family members kindly. Take time to speak to people clearly and to explain yourself. Don't talk down to others or talk about them behind their backs. Resist the temptation to be argumentative, defensive or scheming. There are billions of computer programs out there. You don't have to agree or condone what another person's program believes or does, but you do have to have respect for everyone's path in life, regardless of where it takes them.

#### *Respect your boundaries and those of others:*
Don't accept people's emotional garbage or imposition on your physical space. Don't allow anyone to abuse you in any way. Just as important, remember to avoid doing these things to others. Create

boundaries of time at work and use your boundaries to create balance in your life. Practice saying no (and yes) when you want to.

*Learn to cultivate dedication, discipline, desire, and will:*
Make a list of the things that are important for you to accomplish daily and rate them numerically. Cut out whatever can be removed (those things that are not bringing you absolute happiness, unless they are non-negotiable obligations). Remove all useless activities like habitual behaviors, useless routines, and "doings," which are actions that sabotage your progress. Regardless of what your program says you should do, if you don't desire it with all your heart, don't put it on the list. Start by putting things on the list that you know you can dedicate yourself to without too much effort. When you decide something is important enough to you, you will simply take action and do it.

*Count to ten:*
When you start getting impatient, count to ten, take a deep breath, and have awareness of what is going on. Just by having the clarity to see how your program is trying to abuse you in the moment and what it's saying to you is enough to stop you from losing your patience. Take action and let go of your frustration.

*Appreciate your experience of life:*
Possessing gratitude implies taking action. You can do this by making a habit of thanking yourself and Spirit for your day every day, no matter what has transpired. To do this, you need to constantly forgive yourself and others — it's an ongoing affair. Gratitude and forgiveness are practiced simultaneously for the best effect!

*See the blessings and beauty of life:*
Take the action of setting aside a moment here and there throughout your day to appreciate grace operating in your life. Grace is magic in action. Have the eyes to see what is truly important and meaningful in this reality.

*Practice opening your heart:*
If you keep taking the action of re-focusing your attention on your heart, you will realize how often you're not living your life from that place. Prove to yourself that love doesn't hurt and that your supply is not limited by giving it away as often as possible, until you're able to live your life with a completely open heart. The payoff on this one is huge, I promise!

# Chapter 16

# Transforming Perfectionism Into Acceptance

*One of the more challenging* aspects of our program is its need to attain perfection in a way that's not possible. We never seem to be good enough for ourselves, never mind anyone else! If we ask why this is so and where such a need comes from, the answer lies in our domestication. When we were children, we were always striving to be "good" in order to get our parents' attention and love. Maybe when your parents saw your report card they would say, "Well how come you got a B in math? You should have gotten an A." Or perhaps it was, "You should have made the swim team; you are better than all those other guys." As an adult, it's not a school grade or team you are competing for anymore; it might be a promotion at work instead. Maybe you are trying to "keep up with the "Joneses" or the other people in your social circle, or perhaps you're trying to juggle your job, two kids, your partner, your exercise routine, and the house. We're always trying to reach a certain goal of perfection, but the weird thing is the more we strive for the goal of a perfectly balanced life, the further away it seems to get! The reason is because that kind of perfection just doesn't exist. It's an illusion. To strive for that level of idealism only causes pain and unhappiness, not only in our own lives, but also in the lives of others whom we judge according to our program's particular ideals of perfection.

To have a happy life, it's necessary to overhaul our understanding of perfection and instead endeavor for acceptance. The universe is perfect as it is; the problem is that we're often unable to see life that way because our program is constantly judging and comparing every moment of every experience. As long as we're invested in our program's image of perfection, we'll always be comparing everything to that ideal, which is always shifting forward. As soon as we've reached one "goal," the next one is right there ahead of us. You finally got the big house, for example, but now you need

> "Absolute perfection is here and now, not in some future, near or far. The secret is in action — here and now. It's your behavior that blinds you to yourself. Disregard whatever you think yourself to be and act as if you were absolutely perfect — whatever your idea of perfection may be. All you need is courage."
>
> — SRI NISARGADATTA MAHARAJ

to decorate and put in a pool. And once you reach those goals, you'll be on to something else. It doesn't end with the things that surround us, either. This applies to the way we view ourselves too — plastic surgeons are very busy these days, and the diet and exercise industries are booming for a reason. We're always running after the proverbial carrot, in search of whatever will make us feel "perfect."

> *Consider removing "it should be" from your speech. When you say things should be, must be, need to be, or have got to be a certain way, as opposed to how they are, let this be a flashing red light for you. I should be, my boss should be, my house needs to be, and my partner must be are all spam; all of these phrases demonstrate the expectations of your programming. Look carefully at whether those "should be's" are moving you in the direction of the ever-elusive carrot of perfection. Practice being grateful for what is.*

Acceptance, of ourselves and of life, is the way to counteract the desire for this illusory perfection. Many people feel that if we just accept things as they are, we won't have the impetus to improve ourselves or to make the world a better place to live. But this isn't so. Normally, our motivation is monetary or comes from the desire to acquire more things or a higher status, according to the dictates of our program. The need for things and the drive for perfection creates competition and separation between people. If we're motivated by our desire to be creative, to be happy, and to discover what it means to be the best human we can be, we will do so not because of some image in the mind, but because of the desire in our hearts as an expression of Spirit. Our whole existence on the planet would shift and improve as our incentives in life would change to be more in line with our integrity and hearts. If you accept life on life's terms, you are accepting Spirit in action in your life and that's perfect.

> *Acceptance of one's life has nothing to do with resignation; it does not mean running away from the struggle. On the contrary, it means accepting it as it comes, with all the handicaps of heredity, of suffering, of psychological complexes and injustices.* — PAUL TOURNIER

It's important to note that as a society, we're not a very accepting bunch; indeed, we're quite rigid and controlling. We like to have control over the way things are done and the way they turn out, control over who enters or exits our lives (as if we could actually control when our loved ones pass away or when partners decide they need to leave us), control over whether we're fired or how the economy is functioning, control over how the soda bottles are aligned in the refrigerator and how the shirts are arranged in the closet! Telling everyone around us what to do and how to do it seems to be a national pastime —computer programs trying to be in control of other computer programs! Imagine what life would be like if you chose to change that behavior, and rather than fighting everything in your life, you surrendered to it.

Years ago, I realized that I had been fighting life for so many years I didn't even realize I was doing it. Life was trying to take me in one direction and I was still pushing to go in another direction. I never acknowledged the amount of resistance I had to all of life's circumstances. Guess what? Life always wins! And so do we, if we stop fighting. Surrender is acceptance in action. Once we decide to accept life on life's terms, we can surrender and let go. When we surrender, we let the universe guide us and show us our choices. But just because we surrender doesn't mean we sit around and let life happen to us. Not at all! Life presents us with choices all the time, but once we pick one, we accept that choice and surrender without worrying about it anymore. This is just like reaching a fork in the road. Will we go left or right? It's our choice; we have to pick a direction and then surrender to fate. What good is it to say, "I should have done this or that," or, "What if I took that road instead of this one?"

> *Life is like a river, quiet and smooth in some stretches and roiling, raging and twisting in others — but it only goes in one direction. Try rowing backwards on a raging river. You'll be exhausted in five minutes and will have gone nowhere. Trying to make your partner stay in a relationship that they're finished with it is like rowing backwards. So is trying to make the people you love change, telling your kids what to be when they graduate, and directing your employees how to do every little aspect of their job. The truth is that any feeling of safety you have through taking these actions is just an illusion anyway. You can paddle your boat on the river thinking you are in control, but if you pull the oars in, you'll still be moving. The best way to navigate life is by putting your oars in the water to steer yourself from time to time when it's necessary. Other than that keep the oars in the boat and get out of your own way.*

Life doesn't judge which direction is right or wrong, only we can do that according to what we believe. If you're not having fun going one direction, then take responsibility for your choice and keep your eyes open for the next fork in the road. Then take action again, make a new choice, and keep going. When you participate actively in the process of acceptance and surrender, you retain all the energy you would have wasted fighting and trying to control your way. Believe me, life only happens on life's terms, not yours. There's no room here for bargaining or negotiation!

The last thing I would like to share with you in this chapter is about detachment. In the West, detachment seems to be a bit of a dirty word. People interpret it as being cold, unloving, and separate from those we care about. But Eastern philosophy uses the concept of detachment in a totally different manner, to create clarity in life, to be able to see the forest for the trees, so to speak. When we're detached from the people we love, we see them as individuals who have their own paths in life and their own agendas. We know these people may come and go in our lives and we wish them well. Neediness, clinging, and selfishness prevent us from being detached. We need a little space between us to be able to see our relationships clearly. If we're needy and have to have the people we love the way we want them, we're not respecting them. If we truly love unconditionally, we're able to give our loved ones the space they need to be themselves. In doing so, we give ourselves the same gift! It's a misconception in our society that love must equal need. True love is unconditional and without attachment — period.

Detachment applies to anything we do in life. For instance, I always wanted to do everything the way I wanted, and I needed to be able to control the outcome of all my actions. I realized I was draining a lot of energy doing this, so one day I decided to discuss the issue with my teacher. I begged him to tell me how I could stop being such a control freak. I told him, "I am so tired of my own behavior and I want to change. I just don't know what to do for myself." As usual, he laughed at me with all the love in his heart and said, "Well the answer is very simple. Just be the best control freak you can be," and he walked away!

As you can imagine, this wasn't what I wanted to hear; in fact, I was about to burst into tears when my friend Stephen came along and asked me what was wrong. I explained what had just happened and how angry and upset I was with don Miguel. I was convinced that he didn't want me to change and wanted to see me stay the way I was! Stephen said, "Sheri, all he is saying is do your best in any activity you are engaged in. Once you do that, there is nothing else to be done. You are finished — detach. You can let go and let life take care of the rest. That is what don Miguel was trying to tell you. Don't distort what he's saying and use it to get yourself more upset!" I laughed at myself for working myself up into a dither and thanked Stephen for his very wise words.

> *It's important to understand that detachment is not to be used as an escape from feeling emotions or as an excuse for not opening your heart 100 percent. It has nothing to do with being "cold," as we said before. Please don't distort the practice of detachment to support your unwillingness to go into the dark places in your mind or to avoid fully participating in your life. This would be using the concept of detachment to sabotage and hurt yourself and to avoid confronting the things you need to. Again, honesty and self-reflection are important here to keep the denial system at bay.*

Remember, unconditional love lives in the space between people and things. Be detached from the objects, events, and people in your life and have the clarity and vision to see things as they really are. Let life open itself to you and be available to see what it's showing you. Make the choice to actively participate in life. After all, you have free will, remember? The most important thing I can share with you is that the free will that Spirit gives you allows you only one true choice: Will you live a life of heaven by accepting and surrendering to life, or one of hell, of fighting for control and resistance to life?

*Action list to support the practice of transforming perfection into acceptance:*

### Practice letting go:
Do your best at whatever task you're involved in and then don't look back. Detach from your program's expectations of the way things should turn out. Every reaction to your actions is a sign from the universe. Rather than complaining about outcomes, shift gears and take a new action if the outcome is not what you intended.

### Practice detachment in relationships:
When a loved one leaves you or passes away, take time to grieve for your loss but then detach and move on. Take action to thank that person for the wonderful contribution they made to your life and everything you learned about yourself from their interactions with you. Creating a ritual to celebrate the relationship and its place in your life will help you process the experience more fully and detach much sooner.

### Practice detachment at work:
When you make a presentation or a proposal, let go after you're through. Watch what life does with your work and be ready to change at a moment's notice. Surrender and accept the things that happen and detach from your program's hopes and wishes. If you're fired, for example, accept it gracefully and surrender to your fate. Thank the universe for the opportunity to explore bigger and better things, because you wouldn't have left unless you were let go or things got really intolerable.

### Observe the signs of life:
Every day, take notice of how life is constantly trying to tell you things. If you stop thinking so much about the way things should be, you'll have more clarity regarding what is. You'll automatically be able to make clearer choices with a lot less effort.

# Chapter 17

## *Inviting Fun Into Your Life And Kicking Toxic Energy Out!*

*In our work-driven,* I-want-everything-now society, we never seem to have enough time just to enjoy ourselves and play. Some of my friends don't even know what to do with themselves when they finally have time off! For life to be interesting and stimulating, you must take responsibility for creating that in your life. No one will do it for you. Pretend you don't have the human concept of tomorrow. What are you going to do to make today fantastic? Remember, everything starts with self-love, and taking charge of your fun quotient is definitely an act of love for yourself.

It's so easy to get caught up with the everyday doings of life that by the end of the day all you've accomplished is work, errands, chauffeuring, cooking, and cleaning. A little bit of fun each day will make you feel less resentful of all those other people in your life who are pulling on your time. (No use getting angry at them; they didn't set your schedule up the way it is, you did. Remember how we discussed taking responsibility for your life in Chapter 10? This is responsibility in action.) Only you can create balance in your life and make it the way you want it to be. Don't wait for tomorrow or for someone else to do it for you. You have to make the choice yourself.

Make a priority list of things you want to do for your own enjoyment. Have you ever considered taking art lessons, riding a horse, learning to cook, sew, crochet, knit or do crafts? Or what about dancing or singing lessons, jewelry design, candle or soap making, furniture making, clothing design, or boating? Ever wanted to fly a kite or even a plane — or jump out of one? Learning to windsurf or kite board sounds delightful, or perhaps water-skiing is your thing. Visit a museum, exhibition, street fair, antique store, art gallery, or some cute shops. Get a new hairstyle, have your nails done, have a massage, or take a makeup lesson. Start a book club, gym,

> "We live in a wonderful world that is full of beauty, charm and adventure. There is no end to the adventures that we can have if only we seek them with our eyes open."
>
> —— *JAWAHARLAL NEHRU*

wine tasting group, hiking or biking club or community service organization. Join a softball league or a basketball game. Take some classes or workshops and attend some interesting lectures. Get the degree you always wanted. Learn to enjoy quiet time, join a spiritual group or explore some new philosophies. Go on a vacation you would never think to do in the past, like a hiking trip or culinary travel adventure. Perhaps participating in a spiritual journey, rather than just hitting the beach for a week, would be more enlightening. Maybe something quiet like catching up on some good books, learning to meditate, or doing Yoga sounds good to you.

> *Pick one new activity each month and give it a try. Don't judge it, just do it. Trying something new is like tasting a vegetable or an unusual food for the first time — and remember what your mother told you: "You don't know if you like something until you try it!" You may need to try something a couple of times before you develop a taste for it.*

Make sure to create your list so that it's reasonable in nature; in other words, don't try to take action and accomplish everything on the list all at once unless you want to purposely fail. And if you're not taking action about something you think you should be doing, then stop complaining about it! Do it, change it, or be quiet about it until you're ready to take action. Create a life of vitality, verve, diversity and magic. Use your love for yourself, your dedication, and discipline to get yourself jump started into having an entirely new and exciting life.

In creating a beautiful, fun-filled life, you have the opportunity to censor out a majority of the noxious energy that comes your way, whether it's someone yelling at you, sending their poison or spam your way, or being in the presence of a group of angry people. If someone wants to yell at you, you don't have to participate in that type of communication in any way. Remove yourself with kindness and offer to continue the conversation when that person is prepared to speak to you calmly. Watch for the type of energy that surrounds you and if you're in the presence of people who are agitated, angry, judgmental, or rude, take responsibility for your life and your happiness and leave.

> *One thing that made a huge difference in my own life was to stop cursing. Growing up in NYC, I developed a habit of peppering my communications with four-letter adjectives; until I realized the particular type of energy those words carry with them. By utilizing those words, I was polluting the "air waves" with toxic energy, even if I personally meant no malice. By eliminating those words from my vocabulary — and limiting my exposure to other people who curse — my environment changed. It was amazing!*

Another way toxic energy enters our lives is through the media. Is it necessary to have the TV on all day with the news station running? Do we really need to hear the same reports of war, destruction, hate, sickness, fear, and doom over and over again throughout the course of the day? The same goes for watching soap operas and shows that demonstrate how humans fill their lives with drama, anger, vindictiveness, and jealousy. Subconsciously, we're receiving the message that this is the appropriate emotional way to respond to life's situations. When you invite this energy into your life, you are a willing participant to it. Before you know it, you're giving your happiness away and feeling despondent and depressed.

An interesting thing happened at the time of 9/11 when I was working for my teacher. We had a spiritual journey to Mexico scheduled for several days after the 11th. Of course, we didn't know if the government would allow air travel and all the trip participants were waiting for word on whether we would be going or not. Finally, we realized that there were enough airports open to allow our trip to go on as planned. The group immediately divided into two camps: One group made all kinds of arrangements to get themselves to Mexico. The second group, on the other hand, was very angry that we could even think of leaving the United States. They felt we needed to be home supporting our country, not going off to have "fun" someplace. I truly didn't anticipate this difference of opinions! My personal feeling was that my presence in front of the TV and radio, day after day, watching and listening to all of the reports of carnage and the expressions of fear, would not change anything in a life-affirming way. To me, it would be as if the terrorists had won, with fear triumphing over compassion and love.

> *After 9/11, the stock market went down, the recession got worse, people lost their jobs, and the economy took a nosedive. To me, it seems that the terrorists succeeded in doing exactly what they wanted — not because of their actions, but because of our fears, because of the way we chose to react to the events of that day. We stopped spending money, we let employees go, and we stopped traveling. We've discussed this throughout the book, but it bears repeating here: Fear-based emotions are an incredibly powerful form of fear-based energy!*

I found that journey to be the most energetically intense trip I've ever gone on. The members of our group were so determined to find their own happiness within and bring it back home that the energy of love on the trip was indescribable. The journey, in fact, was a metaphor for our lives: Every moment is filled with choice; how you react to the people in your life and everything that happens is up to you. That is true transformation of toxic energy into compassion, love, and happiness — a re-writing of those infected files in our programming.

*Action list to support the practice of learning to*
*limit and transform your exposure to toxic energy:*

### Turn off the television:

Cutting your viewing time will decrease the amount of news and drama that enters your home. Pay attention to the types of programs you watch and ask yourself if they dramatize the type of situations and communications you want to remove from your life.

### Make your home a "no drama" zone:

With the participation and consent of your other family members, make the choice to declare your home a "no drama zone." This means you decide that there's only love, respectful communication and kindness demonstrated in your home, rather than arguing, bickering, controlling behaviors, and dramatic emotional outbursts.

### Record yourself speaking:

It's shocking to listen to yourself speak! Take action to record yourself communicating on the phone or at home to friends and family and at work. Record an argument between you and your loved ones. Listen to the type of language you use, the feeling behind the words, and the kind of energy you send out. Do you curse, complain, whine, gossip, worry, manipulate, yell, tease, or bicker? Keep doing this exercise until you can feel your voice transmitting love and kindness.

### Make a list of your toxic activities:

What kinds of activities do you engage in that do not support your happiness? If you're in an environment or situation that goes against you, get out! Make an action list of the steps you need to take to make that happen, even if it means changing jobs, limiting the hours you spend with certain people, or cutting certain people out of your life entirely — with all the love in your heart, of course.

*Integrate some fun into your life:*

Make a list of activities that interest you. Don't eliminate anything just because it's not what you would normally do or because you might be afraid or embarrassed. That's just your program trying to spam you by defining the limits of who you are. Don't believe it! You and you alone must take those walls down by trying new things and exploring the full potential of life's possibilities. You will expand your life exponentially every time you experiment and take a chance.

# Chapter 18

## *Establishing Community With Compassion And Kindness*

*One of the most helpful things* for me on my path was the availability of people with the same goal (to overcome their programming) to be there for me when the going got rough — and it was rough often, believe me! A spiritual community is a place where we can experiment with expressing unconditional love and with different kinds of supportive communication. In such a setting, we all are speaking a similar language based in respect and kindness. We can feel comfortable in expressing ourselves knowing that the other members of the group are practicing learning how to listen more effectively. Of course, there's a learning curve here and we or other members in the group may slip into our old ways, but at least we can catch ourselves without judgment or criticism.

*"We must become the change we want to see."*

—*MAHATMA GANDHI*

The way the mind normally works is to befriend people who will support our program's particular point of view so we can be right. The type of community I am talking about brings you together with different people who will challenge your point of view and make you question what you believe about everything. If you're in a group that supports your pity party, for example, then you're in the wrong place. The purpose of a spiritual community is to question the reality of everything and to see the truth behind all of the false concepts that society has given us. It's easier to hear your own virus-corrupted beliefs when they are coming out of another person's mouth. Again, this is about having clarity and seeing what is true rather than what we want to see. The most important thing is to never be part of a group of programs in collusion. Find a group of people who support the spiritual expression of the real you and who don't support the strength of your program by empowering it with the agreement of other infected programs.

Being in a community is also wonderful for those times when you need to have a good cry. Rather than supporting your drama, members of your community can assist you in moving through your emotional time with grace and will support your process rather than supporting your corrupted program and your victimization!. It's wonderful to be around people who will reflect back to you what you believe so you can shift your experience in directions you might never have considered before.

The number one guideline in a group like this is to refrain from telling others what to do or how to do it. Being part of a spiritual community isn't about perpetrating your own program's point of view (and spamming others in the process). Instead, it's about asking questions until the other person can see the light and figure things out for themselves. The second guideline is never to judge another, but to be supportive and listen with an open heart. It doesn't matter what you think of another person in your spiritual group or what you think of their situation or what you would do in their place. You can learn what it's like to support another human being without supporting their point of view. There is a huge difference between the two!

If there is no such community in your area, create one. Get a group of people together who want to better themselves and make a difference in their own lives. Using clear communication between members of your group, set guiding principles designed to support your growth. For example, in addition to the two guidelines discussed above, you could propose that anything discussed in the group stays in the group, that there will be no gossiping in sacred space, or that whomever is speaking gets to tell their whole story without anyone interrupting them (something that will help to develop listening skills that are in short supply these days). Whatever guidelines you decide on, make sure they're for the group's higher good and with the blessing and support of all its members.

> *I shall pass through this life but once. Any good, therefore, that I can do or any kindness I can show to any fellow creature, let me do it now. Let me not defer or neglect it. For I shall never pass this way again.*
>
> — *ÉTIENNE DE GRELLET*

When we start our journey down the path of self-discovery, we spend a lot of time going inside ourselves. It's easy to become self-absorbed and forget about the world around us. Helping others helps us see the commonality of the human experience. And often, it's the little things that make the biggest difference in another person's life, like offering to run an errand for your elderly neighbor or calling to check up on a friend. Doing kind things for others helps make our world a more beautiful place to be and helps to transform the toxic energy around us, something we discussed in Chapter 17.

We must be wise in our actions to "help" others because we don't know what life's experience will be for them. It's not our place to interfere in their path. The best way to help another is to help them to help themselves. Be present, give your love and support them when they take action, but don't take it upon yourself to fix something in their life or interfere in their business. Can you see the difference?

> *While engaging in acts of kindness, make sure your Intent is coming from the desire to promote the higher good of the other person; otherwise, this can turn into an activity to fuel your self-importance, and that will not help anyone, especially not yourself. (Self-importance is the number one obstacle to your personal freedom!)*

If we desire understanding, love, and forgiveness from others, then it behooves us to give the same to them. Compassion is the deep awareness of the suffering of others and the wish to relieve it. By having compassion for others, we can have tolerance for them when they're engaged in their harmful behavior patterns and emotional reactions. We don't have to agree with them, but we can clearly see what's going on and not allow ourselves to be pulled into their tragedy. If you can see why your mom is trying to involve you in her drama, for example, you can have compassion for her behavior and not argue with her or participate in her histrionics. After all, the reason she is upset is probably not because of something that's happening in her life right now, but because of something that has happened in her past. Since you're the one who now has clarity about how the mind works, use this opportunity to practice exercising compassion.

Having compassion does not mean passing judgment, nor does it involve telling someone else how to change their life. Being a compassionate person does not mean you can get upset about someone else's situation and take it to heart. If you do that, you are letting that situation take your happiness away, and that's not the purpose of this activity. Being compassionate assists us in seeing that there is only one life and the action of helping others and having compassion for them ultimately benefits ourselves.

## *Action list to support the practice of establishing community with compassion and kindness.*

### Create your own group:

If there are no spiritual communities in your area, then take action to create your own group. Use the information given here to design your group guidelines or contact my web site (http://www. sherirosenthal.com) for additional help.

### Practice being a mirror:

Take action to reflect the love and wonder that exists in all human beings back to them. Be present among people whose programs are different from yours. Experience different points of view so you can see your own more clearly. Listen carefully, speak sparingly, and question everything.

### Do one kind thing a day:

Make it a daily habit to do at least one thing to help another person or to show compassion. Let someone cut into traffic ahead of you, hold an elevator for another, bring a friend a cup of coffee, send a card to a dear buddy, call someone in need, take your dog to a nursing home, bring a meal to a sick person's house or make sure your elderly neighbor is OK. Volunteer time, help on a committee, smile at people, and take time to understand another person's situation.

# Chapter 19

## *Cultivating The Experience Of Spirit In Your Life*

*Spirit's moving at the speed of light* through every moment of our lives and is changing everything around us. Yet we insist that things stay the same by resisting change in our lives. We get scared and worried and try to hold onto things that no longer belong in our lives, like people, jobs, and possessions. Why are we so frightened of change when change is the only thing that is guaranteed?

To participate fully and absolutely in life, we must live each and every moment like it's our last and only one on earth. By this, I don't mean that you have to strive to accomplish everything in one day because you may not be here tomorrow to get things done. Enjoy each day to the fullest, do your best, and enjoy yourself. Whatever you get done, you get done, but don't worry about it. Don't concern yourself with the past; if you made a mistake, forgive yourself and detach from it. Learn from your errors so that your future is more effortless. Once the moment is gone, you can't change anything anymore, and it's time to let go. And what about the future? You can only take action to the best of your abilities regarding what is to come. And that future will come fast enough without rushing toward it and worrying about it!

> "I am the taste in the water, the light of the sun and the moon, the sound in the ether, the ability in man, the fragrance of the earth, the heat in the fire, the life of all that lives, the strength of the strong, the intelligence of the intelligent, and the original seed of all existences."
>
> —BHAGAVAD GITA

*Be flexible and ready to change in every moment in response to the clues that life is giving you. If you're not fully present, you won't have the eyes or clarity to see all of the opportunities that life's presenting to you right now. Your program will not be able to recognize and integrate those opportunities because your virus-ridden beliefs and old behavior patterns have total control of your attention. You need to shift your attention out of your program into your heart and your Spirit to be able to perceive new and different input. You can't process information that you're not capable of perceiving!*

The more you create space for Spirit in your life the easier it will be to detach from believing you are your mind. The reason for this is obvious, seeing yourself as the magnificent being of light that you are, as total love, will make any nonsense that your mind tries to spam you with you look silly in comparison. The trick is how to do that! Developing faith in yourself and your ability to transcend the chatter of the mind is a good place to start.

Take time to meditate, quiet time in which you practice silencing your mind. In these moments, even if at first you can only be quiet for a second, try to connect with your heart and the beauty of the world around you. Experience the oneness of life around you. There are many forms of meditation and tons of classes available. When I first tried to meditate, I found that I couldn't quiet my mind and breathe at the same time. During my difficult childhood, being able to anticipate my parents' activities and needs were paramount to my survival. Thinking was breathing! It took months of listening to tapes involving breath work for my body to realize I would not die if I stopped thinking. But again, discipline, dedication, and desire (things we discussed in Chapter 15) always win out in the end.

Meditative walking (like a long walk or hike in the woods or along a lake) is also a lovely activity. Immersing yourself in nature is akin to immersing yourself in Spirit; after all, they're one and the same. Seeing the beauty around you allows you to be able to experience the beauty in yourself. Yoga is another form of contemplation. The intense concentration required to hold the poses makes it necessary to quiet the mind and focus on the body and Spirit. The meaning of Yoga is union-discipline and the union we're speaking of is mind, body, and Spirit.

> *Love the moment and the energy of the moment will spread beyond all boundaries.*
> — CORITA KENT

Another fairly simple practice is to put yourself into silence. Devote one day a week or even half a day to silence. (You can even engage your children in this practice.) A silent retreat is a wonderful vacation choice. Everything slows down as you detach from the laundry list of things that hook your mind in your daily life. I remember my first few spiritual journeys with my teacher. Since I believed that I knew everything, I couldn't imagine not putting my two cents into whatever conversation I was privy to. The first thing he did on the trip was to put me into silence for three days. It was sheer torture! Being silent was like quitting cigarettes cold turkey. I kept quiet, thinking of all the perfect things I could add to the conversations so people could see how brilliant and witty I was, if only I could say one thing. I could barely sit still while people were speaking, and believe me, they were definitely enjoying themselves at my expense. By the third day, I had the amazing revelation that none of things I wanted to say was of any real importance or significance. Everything was just my opinion, my judgment, my point of view. And twenty years from now all of my conversations will be lost in the dust. I saw that nothing really matters except my love for others and myself. Most of what we call conversation is just a bunch of useless, mindless spam and chatter, filled with complaining, gossiping, and story-telling.

The creation of an altar is an excellent way to express yourself spiritually and is a lovely self-gift. If you create the altar intellectually, trying to figure out the proper decorating choice for the look of your altar or trying to make a "correct" altar, you'll defeat its purpose. I love my altar and I have spent quite a bit of time in front of it. When times were tough, I prayed there. When the universe sent me a sign or a token (a feather found during a contemplative walk, or the perfect message inside my fortune cookie), I put it on my altar. I've placed symbols of the issues I was working on in my life (challenges regarding work, finances or relationships) on my altar. It became a living picture of the spiritual life I was creating for myself and for my personal process and transformation. It has been a refuge, a confidant, and a friend.

> *There is no "right" way to create an altar; all you need is a small space (my altar is on my dresser), your heart, and your imagination. Let your altar be a very personal living, breathing, and changing expression of you.*

We're often so tied up in our lives that we lose the ability to see Spirit around us and in us at all moments. That is why it's important to cultivate these qualities in ourselves and engage in activities that will continually remind us of who we really are. Nothing is stopping us from taking action in moving forward toward self-love, personal freedom, and a magical life except a self-defeating, self-sabotaging, spam-filled, corrupted, virus-ridden program.

Earlier in this book I shared the concept of faith being the force that life uses to manifest itself (Intent in Toltec terms). Our personal Intent is a smaller version of the monumental force that exists throughout the universe pushing forth and directing the creation of life. It's a gift from Spirit and that's why it's so important to have clarity on where and into what things our Intent is invested. This is a different way of thinking about faith than what we're used to in our Western thinking. Most of us who have a Judeo-Christian background can recognize that what we really have is blind faith. We believe in something just because our Priest, Minister, Rabbi, or religious writings ask us to. In the Toltec philosophy, we're asked to experience divine consciousness directly, without the computer program, so we can have an intimate knowing of Spirit. The purpose of this is to make our faith absolute — not because of something we have learned, heard, or read but because we have the personal experience of it within ourselves. When we're able to do this, our faith is no longer blind.

> *You can have anything you want if you want it enough. You must want it with an inner exuberance that erupts through the skin and joins the energy that created the world.* — SHEILA GRAHAM

When I invest my faith in my computer program and its spam, my life becomes very one-dimensional. Limitations are everywhere, confusion sets in, and things become difficult, weary, and boring. When I take my faith out of my computer program and put it into Spirit and the beauty of creation that lives within my heart, life becomes holographic, expansive and limitless. Opportunities are everywhere, life is easy and joyful, and clarity is the order of the day.

You can't put your faith and personal power in the files of your computer program and in Spirit. It just doesn't work that way. You need to make a commitment one way or another. Most of us are totally invested in what we believe about ourselves and our world, but to be totally free, we must put our faith into life completely. This is absolute personal freedom — as no man can serve two masters.

And so it is. There's really no way to tell someone how to do this; there's no instruction manual. You need to just keep walking on your path, be present in your life, and keep listening to your heart. Miracles happen every moment of every day, whether you believe it or not! Our society dream is simply an illusion that takes all of our attentions away from the truth of what we really are — divine.

*Action list to support the practice of learning to create the experience of Spirit in your life:*

### Be here now:

Set a stop watch to ring every hour on the hour. When the stop watch goes off, ask yourself if you are in the same place mentally and emotionally as you were an hour ago. Use the alarm to re-direct your attention to the present and break your habit of making situations that are happening right now look like ones that happened years ago. If so, detach and move on; believe me — life already did!

### Practice meditation:

If you have no time to sit and meditate quietly, do it while taking a long drive, walking the dog, washing dishes, ironing, on your way to the gym or work or even while sitting on the toilet! Listen to a guided meditative tape or relaxing music or nothing at all, other than your heart beating and your breathing. Resist the temptation to fill that time with regular music or the news and instead make time for your relationship with yourself.

### Put your mind's computer in hibernation mode:

By practicing silence, you will quiet the noisy computer of your mind and the resultant spam. I encourage you to make this part of your action plan. With the computer on hibernate, you'll feel the real you, Spirit, and the opening of your heart rather than the churning of your mind's programming.

### Dream a beautiful altar:

Don't let your program tell you this is a silly activity. Express your Spirit self with this wonderful ritual that humanity has used for thousands of years. Involving your loved ones in this activity can help encourage the expression of Spirit in your home and involve your family in your process rather than excluding them. You may surprise yourself with the results.

# Postscript

*The path to self-discovery* does not end with this book. There are so many opportunities and resources out there to avail yourself of; you just have to take the first step. It's not necessary to have money. You can form a group of friends who want to make the commitment to change themselves and their lives. You can check my web site (listed below) for additional information on our community forum and other fun activities.

If it's within your means, come join us for a retreat, weekend workshop or even a spiritual journey. Taking the opportunity to remove yourself from your day-to-day life can give you the opportunity to see things more clearly and help you have the actual experience of Spirit within yourself. These experiences assist you in creating and developing faith in yourself and your ability to change your life and your programming. We're all capable, strong people; we just forget this from time to time and need a little help to get motivated. Creating community allows you to perpetuate this experience when you get back home so you don't get lazy or sucked back into your old patterns.

There are many other good books out there that encourage you to take action in your life. Of course, my personal favorites are those books written by my teacher, don Miguel Ruiz. I highly recommend *The Four Agreements*°, *The Mastery of Love,* and *The Voice of Knowledge.* I think you will enjoy them too. Another great book is *The Complete Idiot's Guide To Toltec Wisdom* by yours truly! And if you need some assistance with your forgiveness process you can sign up for the free 52-day forgiveness program at www.withforgivenessmovie.com.

New Thought, Unity, and Religious Science Churches also have lots of activities, classes and discussion groups that support these kinds of teachings. These churches support the universal truth of unconditional love and the one life it emanates from by encouraging us to discover that light within ourselves and our community.

For more information on Sheri's exciting events, mentoring program and workshops — or to sign up for her free newsletter, free weekly audio message and free teleclasses please visit her web sites:

*www.sherirosenthal.com*
*www.withforgivenessmovie.com*

In addition you will find a fantastic community forum, a busy blog, pithy podcasts and a scintillating store! If you are ready to embark on a Spiritual Journey or Retreat, please visit:

*www.journeysofthespirit.com*

I look forward to the opportunity of meeting you and passing along the message of unconditional love, light and joy!

*Blessings along your path, and may your life be filled with*
*the abundance of*
*the wonderment and magic*
*that life has to offer.*
*With all my love,*
*Sheri*

*Que tu sol sea brillante!*
*— May your sun shine brightly! —*

# About The Author

*Sheri Rosenthal,* DPM is a Master Toltec Teacher trained by don Miguel Ruiz (New York Times bestselling author of *The Four Agreements*). For two years she acted as Executive Director of Sixth Sun Foundation, a Toltec non-profit corporation. There Sheri had the opportunity and privilege to design and run don Miguel Ruiz's spiritual journeys, and co-teach with him at his workshops. In her former life, she practiced as a podiatric surgeon and ran a surgical residency program at Northside Hospital in Florida.

Sheri is also the author of *The Complete Idiot's Guide to Toltec Wisdom*, a wonderful book on everything you could want to know about the Toltec tradition. In addition, she has co-created the www.WithForgiveness.com program with her friend Susyn Reeve. She is passionate about spiritual journeys and is owner of Journeys of the Spirit® (www.journeysofthespirit.com) a tour company that specializes in adventures that open the heart and heal the mind.

Over the past years Sheri has had profound experiences that have changed the way she sees reality. It is her goal to share the possibilities of that reality and the light of the divine to all those she meets. Participating in the active creation of the dream of heaven on earth is her idea of personal freedom.

# Notes